PENGUIN BOOKS

THE BIBLE ACCORDING TO SPIKE MILLIGAN
THE OLD TESTAMENT

Spike Milligan was born at Ahmednagar in India in 1918. He received his first education in a tent in the Hyderabad Sindh desert and graduated from there, through a series of Roman Catholic schools in India and England, to the Lewisham Polytechnic. Always something of a playboy, he then plunged into the world of show business, seduced by his first stage appearance, at the age of eight, in the nativity play of his Poona convent school. He began his career as a band musician, but since became famous as a humorous scriptwriter and actor in both films and broadcasting. He was one of the main figures in and behind the infamous *Goon Show*.

Spike Milligan's many books include *Silly Verse for Kids*; *Puckoon*; *Badjelly the Witch*; *The Looney: An Irish Fantasy*; *The Lost Goon Shows*; *It Ends with Magic*; *The Bible According to Spike Milligan: The Old Testament*; *Lady Chatterley's Lover According to Spike Milligan*; *Hidden Words*, a collection of his poems; and *A Children's Treasury of Spike Milligan*. His unique and incomparable seven volumes of war memoirs are *Adolf Hitler: My Part in His Downfall*, *'Rommel?' 'Gunner Who?'*, *Monty: His Part in My Victory*, *Mussolini: His Part in My Downfall*, *Where Have All the Bullets Gone?*, *Goodbye Soldier* and *Peace Work*, all of which are published by Penguin.

Spike Milligan received an honorary CBE in 1992 and an honorary knighthood in 2001. He died in February 2002. On his death the *Guardian* described him as 'a creative writer close in stature to Lewis Carroll and Edward Lear in his command of the profound art of nonsense'. He was, said novelist and comedian Ben Elton, 'one of the last century's true originals … a comic genius'.

THE OLD TESTAMENT

PENGUIN BOOKS

PENGUIN BOOKS

Published by the Penguin Group
Penguin Books Ltd, 80 Strand, London WC2R 0RL, England
Penguin Putnam Inc., 375 Hudson Street, New York, New York 10014, USA
Penguin Books Australia Ltd, 250 Camberwell Road, Camberwell, Victoria 3124, Australia
Penguin Books Canada Ltd, 10 Alcorn Avenue, Toronto, Ontario, Canada M4V 3B2
Penguin Books India (P) Ltd, 11 Community Centre, Panchsheel Park, New Delhi – 110 017, India
Penguin Books (NZ) Ltd, Cnr Rosedale and Airborne Roads, Albany, Auckland, New Zealand
Penguin Books (South Africa) (Pty) Ltd, 24 Sturdee Avenue, Rosebank 2196, South Africa

Penguin Books Ltd, Registered Offices: 80 Strand, London WC2R 0RL, England

www.penguin.com

First published by Michael Joseph 1993
Published in Penguin Books 1994
037

Copyright © Spike Milligan Productions Ltd, 1993
All rights reserved

The moral right of the author has been asserted

Printed in England by Clays Ltd, St Ives plc

ISBN-13: 978–0–140–23970–6

www.greenpenguin.co.uk

❦ CHAPTER I ❦

THE CREATION ACCORDING TO THE

TRADE UNIONS

IN THE BEGINNING GOD CREATED THE HEAVEN AND THE EARTH.

2. And darkness was upon the face of the deep; this was due to a malfunction at Lots Road Power Station.

3. And God said, Let there be light; and there was light, but Eastern Electricity Board said He would have to wait until Thursday to be connected.

4. And God saw the light and it was good; He saw the quarterly bill and that was not good.

5. And God called the light Day, and the darkness He called Night, and so passed His GCSE.

6. And God said, Let there be a firmament and God called the firmament heaven, Freephone 999.

7. And God said, Let the waters be gathered together unto one place, and let the dry land appear, and in London it went on the market at six hundred pounds a square foot.

8. And God said, Let the earth bring forth grass, and the earth brought forth grass and the Rastafarians smoked it.

9. And God said, Let there be lights in heaven to give light to the earth, and it was so, except over England where there was heavy cloud and snow on high ground.

10. And God said, Let the seas bring forth that that hath life, flooding the market with fish fingers, fishburgers and grade-three salmon.

11. And God blessed them, saying, Be fruitful, multiply, and fill the sea, and let fowl multiply on earth where Prince Charles and Prince Philip would shoot them.

12. And God said, Let the earth bring forth cattle and creeping things, and there came cows, and the BBC Board of Governors.

13. And God said, Let us make man in our own image, but woe many came out like *Spitting Image*.

14. And He said, Let man have dominion over fish, fowl, cattle and every creepy thing that creepeth upon the earth.

15. And God said, Behold, I have given you the first of free yielding seed, to you this shall be meat, but to the EC it will be a Beef Mountain.

✧ CHAPTER II ✧

ON THE SEVENTH DAY GOD ENDED HIS WORK, but Datsun of Coventry workers went on to time and a half, and God rested from all His work with complete backing from Arthur Scargill and the miners.

2. God blessed the seventh day, as did all the Pakistani corner shops.

3. Every plant, every herb was in earth for the Good Lord had not caused it to rain; because of this Bob Geldof had to raise fifty million quid with Live Aid.

4. And the Lord formed man of the dust of the ground, and breathed into his nostrils the breath of life; it was done privately and not on the National Health.

5. The Lord planted a Garden in Eden and there He put the man He had formed, and He sold the idea to the BBC as *Gardeners' World*.

6. And out of the ground the Lord grew every tree that was pleasant to the sight, but He had not reckoned on the weather forecast from Michael Fish, and they were all blown down in the hurricane.

7. And the Lord took man and put him in the Garden of Eden to dress it and to keep it, subject to compulsory purchase by Brent Council.

8. The Lord God said of every tree of the garden

thou mayest freely eat, but He was apprehended at the check-out and forced to pay.

9. But of the tree of knowledge, thou shalt not eatest, or thou shall surely die, due to crop-spraying with DDT.

10. And the Lord said, it is not good that man should be alone. He caused a deep sleep to fall on Adam, which the shop steward penalised him for during working hours, deducting a day's pay. The Lord took one of Adam's ribs, and made a woman and brought her unto the man, which immediately qualified for common law wife allowance.

11. And they were both naked, the man and his wife, and were not ashamed. However, at Bow Street they were charged with indecency.

✂️ CHAPTER III ✂️

NOW THE SERPENT WAS MORE SUBTLE THAN BEASTS OF THE FIELD; he said unto woman: 'Come and eat the fruit of this tree.' Woman said, 'Nay, if we eat or touch it we die.' And the serpent said, 'Fear not, they are not from South Africa,' whereupon she ate and gave of it to her husband.

2. And the eyes of them were both opened and they knew they were both naked, and Adam said to her, 'Stand back, I don't know how big this is going to get.'

3. And the Lord God called unto Adam: 'Where are thou?'

4. And Adam said, 'I art here.'

5. But both Adam and Eve's eyes were opened and they saw they were naked and they sewed on fig leaves – one for Eve and a hundred and eighty for Adam.

6. The Lord said, 'Who told thee that thou wast naked?'

7. And Adam said, 'I could see it all hanging down.'

8. 'Has thou eaten of the apple?' said the Lord.

9. 'Yea, Eve gave it to me,' said Adam. 'A Granny Smith.'

10. 'Woman,' said the Lord, 'what hast thou done?'

11. And Eve said, 'I haven't done anything, I've only just got here.'

12. And the Lord said unto the serpent, 'Because thou hast done this, thou art cursed above all cattle, and above every beast of the field; upon thy belly thou shalt go, and dust shalt thou eat all the days of your life.'

13. 'This is victimisation,' said the serpent; 'I shall appeal to the RSPCA.'

14. Unto Adam and Eve the Lord God made coats of skins and, verily, they looked terrible – you could *still* see it all.

15. And Eve saw Cain and said, 'Lo, I have gotten a man from the Lord.'

16. And she got another son and together they were called Cain and Abel.

17. And it came to pass that Cain rose up and slew Abel very badly.

18. And the Lord said, ''Ello, 'ello, 'ello, what's going on 'ere?'

19. And the Lord set a mark upon Cain – it was on his right forearm and said Man. United.

20. And Cain went out from Eden to the land of Nod, but there was a curse on the land; it was called Nationwide Building Society.

21. And Cain knew his wife and she bore him a child, Enoch, and in the goodness of time they were all in B&B.

22. But Cain was wise and applied for child benefit.

23. And Adam lived one hundred and thirty years after a course of male hormones. He was lifted on and off and, lo, he begat a son, Seth, who went on to begat

many sons and daughters and won the Queen's Award for Industry.

24. Seth lived one hundred and five years and, after testosterone tablets, begat Enos.

25. And it came to pass, men began to multiply on the face of the earth – and lo, there were many queues for hip operations and standing only on the tube.

26. And the sons of God saw the daughters of men and they were fair; and they took them wives all of which they chose but, woe, the sleeping arrangements were dodgy.

27. There were giants on the earth in those days; they were all in the British Rugby team.

28. The Lord looked upon the earth and, lo, it was corrupt with *Nightmare on Elm Street III*.

29. He sayeth unto Noah, build an ark and two of every animal of the earth thou shalt take in it. So Noah let the animals in and, lo, Noah and his family were soon up to their necks in it. And Noah's wife said, 'For God's sake – somebody open a window.'

30. And the Lord made it rain forty days and nights and the world was flooded, all except England where they had drought and a hosepipe ban.

31. And the rain and the waters prevailed upon the earth a hundred and fifty days and, woe, cricket was cancelled at the Oval.

32. And it came the waters abated, and Noah sent forth a raven – yea, he went forth and stayed forth.

33. Noah then sent forth a dove and, lo, it returned with an olive leaf plucked off. Noah himself was pretty plucked off.

34. Noah waiteth seven days and he sendeth off the dove yet again – but this time it returned not, having been shot on the Glorious Twelfth.

35. And when the land had dried, Noah lifted the cover off the ark and let it all out.

36. And Noah built an altar for the Lord with DIY and gave a burnt offering. But the Lord was angry and said, 'This offering is burnt.' So Noah sweareth and doeth it all over again in the microwave.

37. And Noah went forth with his wife and sons, and they planteth a vineyard. Soon Noah was drunk as a newt.

38. And Ham saw the nakedness of his father and was jealous of the size. For it was there for all to see, and Ham told his two brethren.

39. And Shem and Japheth took a garment, and went backward and covered the nakedness; and their faces were backward, and they walketh over a cliff.

40. Then Noah awoke from the wine – and saw some joker had tied a blue ribbon round it and he hideth it with his hands.

41. And all the days of Noah were nine hundred and fifty years, the last three hundred on a zimmer. Lo, he died of deafness; there was a horse and cart coming up behind him and he heareth it not.

42. And so the children of Noah begat many children and they too begat children – everywhere, behind every bush, they were begatting.

43. But Sarai was barren. She had no children and the Lord put her on to Abram, who did it to her until

he fell off. Then the Lord blessed Abram — but Sarai said, 'Never mind that, get him off.'

44. The Lord said unto Abram, 'Get thee out of the country.' And Abram said, 'What about my mortgage?'

'It will pass,' said the Lord. As he spoke the mortgage went past Abram, so he offered the Lord another burnt offering. The Lord was angry and said this is worse than the M1. Abram was sore afraid and fell on his face and the Lord said, 'Does that hurt?'

Abram said, 'Yes.'

And the Lord said, 'Upsydaisy.'

So Abram upped his daisy.

And the Lord said, 'Now lift up thine eyes, look from the place thou art northward, southward, eastward and westward.'

'It makes me giddy,' said Abram. But in one Biblical bound Abram was free.

45. And Abram said, 'Behold, to me thou hast given no seed.' The word of the Lord came unto him saying, 'This shall not be thine heir.'

'Oh!' said Abram.

And the Lord said, 'But he that shall come forth out of thine own bowels shall be thine heir.'

For months Abram waited, but nothing came out of his bowels. 'How long, O Lord?' said Abram, straining away.

The Lord said, 'Abram, stop thy straining for if it hath not come to pass by now it never will.'

46. When Abram was ninety years and nine, the Lord appeared with painkillers and said unto him,

'Walk before me, and be thou perfect.' But Abram was with rheumatism plus a humpty back and the Lord saw he was far from perfect and put him on BUPA. But, verily, worse was to come.

47. The Lord said, 'Thy name shall be Abraham and Sarai thy wife shall be Sarah. And ye shall be circumcised in the flesh of your foreskin.'

Abraham was afraid and clutched his bits to him.

48. And the Lord spoke from a cloud: 'And every man child and every man of your house will be circumcised.'

'O Lord,' said Abraham, 'where are we going to put it all?'

'Fear not,' said the Lord, 'they are biodegradable and there are many hungry dogs. And the uncircumcised will be cursed and will go forth with it hanging down into the nettles.'

49. The Lord said, 'I will bless Sarah, and she will bear a child by you.'

Then Abraham fell on his face and laughed; many teeth went. 'A child at my age?' said Abraham.

50. 'Abraham,' called the Lord, 'fear not your age; you still have all the bits required. There is an old Jewish proverb, surely as the serpent hisseth and the lamb calls its mother, therefore will the wild horse run its race to the East End.'

'Lord, I don't know what you're talking about,' said Abraham.

'Fear not,' said the Lord, 'thou shalt have a son and his name shalt be Isaac; your wife is stirring the mixture at the moment.'

51. And the Lord appeared on a burning bush but, lo, there was a smell of burning hairs.

52. On the selfsame day was Abraham circumcised and Ishmael his son by Hagar, Sarah's handmaid. And all the men of his house were circumcised; the bits were everywhere, and for many weeks they wore not underpants and there were many screams in the night, and the wives goeth without.

53. And the Lord appeared unto Abraham in the plains of Mamre, which were safer than the planes of Air Uganda. Abraham sat in the tent door in the heat of the day, knackered. He would make a feast for the Lord. He ran into the herd, took a calf and gave it to a butcher who dressed it; it came back wearing shorts, a T-shirt and football boots.

The Lord was well pleased with the joke and said to Abraham, 'Thou shalt have a son.'

Abraham was fearful and afraid as he still had a sore willy. 'But, Lord, I am old, it's all shrivelled up.'

'Fear not,' said the Lord, 'I will unshrivel it, go now and begat.'

54. Abraham went into Sarah and said, 'The Lord wants me to start a nation.'

And Sarah laughed and said, 'You couldn't start a bus.'

55. The brother of Abraham had a son called Lot and he grew up, which is the right direction, and he dwelt near the cities of Sodom and Gomorrah, sinful places where they kerb-crawleth.

56. And the Lord said unto Abraham, 'Because the cry of Sodom and Gomorrah is great, I will go down

now, and see whether they have done altogether according to the cry of it, which is come unto me; and if not, I will know.'

57. 'Eh???' said Abraham.

58. Then Lot spake, 'Up, get out of this place.' Lot's wife sobbed as only that day the new carpet had been fitted.

The Lord appeared in a cloud of something and from somewhere in it said, 'I will destroy this city, it will cost the Halifax dear.'

59. Lot then sayeth what soundeth like a conundrum: 'Behold now, this city is near to flee unto, and it is a little one. Let me escape thither (is it not a little one?)'

And the Lord appeared in a bowl of custard: 'Flee the city, but look not back at the "For Sale" signs.' Then the Lord rained upon Sodom and Gomorrah brimstone, diesel and fire. All the main services came to a halt. Lot of the little one and his wife left, but woe betide! His wife looked back and turned into a pillar of salt. So Lot didn't have to buy salt for the rest of his days.

60. And Abraham rose early to see the city in smoking ruins and sayeth, 'There goes their chance of putting on the Olympics.'

61A. And, with his two daughters, Lot left Zoar where he had fled to, as the prices were too high and he put a deposit on a cane so he layeth down and waiteth for prices to drop.

61B. The one daughter said to the other, 'Our father is old, and there is not a man in the world to come to us.' For Lot there was no disco in the land. The daughters said, 'Let us give our father wine and we will lie with him that we may preserve his seed.' And six nights they did seed saving. Lot said he couldn't remember any of it and was remanded for a psychiatrist's report. Two sons were born; the daughters had given birth to their own brothers, Moab and Benammi.

62. Abraham was now eight hundred years old, by now it had almost dropped off.

63. And the Lord visited Sarah as He had said, and the Lord did unto Sarah as He had spoken. And Sarah delivered a son called Isaac by Red Star. To save money Abraham circumcised him using Mrs Beeton's cookery book as God had commanded him.

64. And there was in the land a woman Hagar who had been using old men's hormones. When Abraham was fourscore and six years old he had put seed unto her and she had borne a son, Ishmael, and when Sarah had heard she had clouteth Abraham good and proper, then she clouted Hagar, and Abraham said, 'Stop, thou knowest not what you do.'

'I know what I'm doing,' said Sarah, 'I'm doing her.'

'Stay your hand,' said Abraham, 'Hagar is only a timeshare wife.' It was only ten minutes.

65. Now, the Lord appeared unto Hagar. He said, 'Arise, lift up your lad, for I will make him a great nation.'

'Anyone but Iraq,' said Hagar.

66. And the lad greweth every day asking, 'Mother, when do I become a great nation?' His mother took him a wife out of the land of Egypt. Seeing this bint, the lad started to begat her. And the Lord saw it and said, 'I

will make you a great nation.' And Hagar said, 'Don't worry, if you want he'll make you one.'

And Abraham went forth and gave seven lambs to Abimelech, and Abimelech said, 'Why do you bring me seven lambs?'

'Because,' sayeth Abraham, 'it's all I've got.'

God did tempt Abraham and said unto him, 'Abraham,' and he said, 'Behold, here am I' and, sure enough, there he was. The Lord said, 'Take thy son, Isaac, take him to the land of Moriah and offer him for a burnt offering.'

'Thou wantest me to make him snuff it?'

'Yea,' said the Lord.

So using breeze blocks, Abraham made a barge, lit the fire and told him to get on it – and Abraham said, 'Lord, do you want anything with him? Chips?'

Abraham was preparing to cook Isaac, who was saying, 'Dad, it's getting hot up here.'

'I'm only obeying orders, son,' said Abraham as he basted Isaac with first cold pressing olive oil, then he took up the carving knife to fricassee his son and an angel of the Lord said, 'Lay not thine hand upon the lad.'

'What's up?' said Abraham. 'Has he gone vegetarian?'

The angel said the Lord is well pleased with you.

'Is that it, then?' said Abraham. And it was.

67. And Sarah died in the Hebron; when they opened the Hebron, there she was on the floor. Abraham wept and sayeth unto his sons, 'Give me a burying place that I may bury my dead out of my sight.'

'You'll have to close your eyes,' they said.

He did and fell in the grave. And his son Isaac said, 'Verily, at your age it's not worth climbing out.'

68. Abraham was old and the Lord had blessed him in all things; indeed, however, by now Abraham's things were well worn. And Abraham said unto his eldest servant, 'I pray thee, put thy hand under my thigh.' And the servant placed her hand under the thigh of her master. And Abraham said, 'The Lord God of heaven, who stopped me frying my son, took me from my father's house and spake unto me etc., saying, unto thy seed will I give this land; he shall send his angels before thee and then shall take a wife unto my son.'

'Can I take my hand out now?' said the servant.

'Thou art a spoilsport,' said Abraham. Then Abraham bowed down before the Lord but it got him in the back. Then Abraham gave all he had unto Isaac including the fish knives and the float in the till. Then he gave up the ghost.

Isaac told the sons, 'He hath snuffed it.' The fees for the cemetery being high they burned him in a cave. 'We must brick up the cave,' said Isaac.

'What for?' said a son. 'Nobody wants to get in.'

'Yes, but we don't want him to get out,' said Isaac.

69. Isaac cried out to the Lord because after lots of begatting his Rebekah was barren, and the Lord intreated of him, and Rebekah conceived. And Isaac was suspicious, but an angel said the Lord works in mysterious ways – and that was one of them.

70. And, lo, Rebekah delivered twins. The first one came out red, all over like an hairy garment; and they called him Esau, then came his brother, who was not

red and hairy. Isaac was sad and said, 'Lord, they don't match.' They called the second one Jacob. Esau grew up to be a hunter – no woman was safe. Jacob grew up and stayed there. Isaac loved Esau because he ate venison, Rebekah loved Jacob because he was a vegetarian.

And Jacob sod pottage, it was called so; when he was a child and they were given pottage for breakfast Isaac would say, 'Sod pottage.'

As Jacob ate his sod pottage, Esau said, 'I'm hungry, give me a mess of sod pottage and I will give you my birthright.' So Jacob took Esau's birthright and a post-dated cheque.

71. And woe there was famine in the land. No matter where you looked it was famine. If you lifted up a chair there it was, if you looked under a bed there it was.

72. And Isaac prostrated himself and said, 'Lord, there is famine, there's even some of it under me.'

The Lord appeared in a cloud but Isaac couldn't see Him as he was face down, and the Lord said, 'Sojourn in this land, and I will be with thee and will bless thee; and unto thy seed and I will perform the oath which I swore unto Abraham.'

'Never mind all that,' said Isaac; 'what we need is rain.'

So Isaac went and dwelt in Gerar. Men there asked him of his wife: 'She is my sister,' said Isaac. He was frightened to say she was his wife in case they killed him to get at her.

But one day the king of the Philistines was peering out a window – he liked a good peer – when, yea, he saw Isaac sporting with Rebekah. Well, it *looked* like sporting. The king was angry and said unto Isaac and Rebekah, 'Put your sports clothes on, she is your wife not your sister, one of my men might lightly had lien with her.'

Isaac turned to Rebekah and said, 'Have you been having any light liening?'

'My lord, nay, I am thine wife,' said Rebekah, and taking his hand placed it on her bosom whereupon Isaac gave it a good squeeze. And the Lord blessed him. Now Isaac sowed the land and in a year received a hundredfold and a rates demand. The Lord blessed him, then blessed him again as it didn't take the first time.

And Isaac waxed great, went forward, because that's where he was going, and he grew until he became very great, eighteen stone, and a hernia — the Lord blessed that too.

73. It came to pass, Isaac's servants told him they had dug a well and said, 'We have found water.' And Isaac called it Shebah. Everyone else called it water.

74. And there came the Philistine Army to make peace. Peace on you, they said, and Isaac said, And peace on you. And he made them a feast. And they rose up betimes of a morning and swore one to another, wake up you dozy bastards.

75. When Isaac was old his eyes were like British Rail employees, dim. The Lord looked into his eyes and said, 'Yea, thine eyes look like dim British Rail employees.'

'Who is there?' said Isaac.

''Tis I, Esau.'

'Pray, make a dinner of venison that I may eat and bless you before I die.'

Rebekah heard this and told her favourite son Jacob, 'You must make a meal so you will be blessed first.'

'But Mother, Father can see the difference. Esau is a hairy man while I am a smooth man,' said Jacob.

'Let me see,' said Rebekah and, true enough, it was smooth. 'Don't worry.' Rebekah gave him this Gorilla-gram skin.

Wearing the skin Jacob took a dinner to Isaac.

'Come, let me feel you,' said Isaac. And he felt.

'Ow, not there, Father,' said Jacob, rehanging them.

'Who art thou?' said Isaac.

'I art Esau, the red and hairy one,' said Jacob.

'Then why does thou smell like a gorilla?' said Isaac.

'It is the will of the Lord,' said Jacob.

Isaac was stricken with wonder as he didn't know the Lord had left a gorilla in His will.

76. When Esau, all red and hairy, returned he was knackered. When he heard what had happened, 'Woe to my father, he didn't get a dinner – he got a Gorilla-gram – woe to the man who knoweth not the difference between a dinner and a Gorillagram.'

And Isaac cursed Jacob, 'You little bastard, there will be a curse on your house – the Halifax Building Society.' And he sent Esau to write 'Burn' on Jacob's roof.

And when Jacob saw it he hid his mother's eyes that she seeth not 'Burn' on the roof. Jacob rose up. 'Thou has defiled mine roof.'

'Ha ha,' said Esau, 'wait till you see what's on the other side.'

And Jacob goeth to the other side and, lo, there was

a four-letter word, and Jacob fled the home and the signs that Esau was making to him.

77. And Jacob goeth and chose a wife: one of the daughters of Heth.

'Which one will thou have?' said Heth.

And Jacob said, 'The one with the big tits.'

And sayeth Rebekah, 'Now my sons have gone, what is there for me to do?'

And Isaac said, 'The laundry.'

And Esau in a red hairy rage did say, 'I will kill my brother.'

And Rebekah said, 'Thou must not.'

'Why not?' said Esau.

'Because it's bad for him,' said Rebekah; 'ever since he was a little boy he's hated being killed.'

78. When Isaac knew what had happened despite the hosepipe ban he raised his eyes to heaven and cried upwards.

And Rebekah said unto Isaac, 'Esau and Jacob leaveth to take wives, woe – what good shall my life do to me?'

And Isaac, who was eight hundred, said, 'You won't be getting it any more.'

And Rebekah said thank God.

79. Jacob went out from Beer-sheba and he lighted upon a certain place and he tarried there, he tarried here, he tarried there, he tarried out the window, he tarried all over the place and, when he'd had enough tarry, using a stone for a pillow he fell asleep, but only with the help of Valium. The Lord worked in mysterious ways and this was one of them. Jacob dreamed of a tall

ladder reaching from heaven to earth — at first he thought it was the escalator at Harrods full of Arab shoplifters, but then he saw they were angels. So Jacob tarried a while, then he got up.

God said, 'Jacob, I'm with thee.'

Jacob said, 'I'm with the Woolwich,' and thought: if God will be with me in this way and will give me bread to eat and raiment to put on, I won't have to sign on again. Then he took his stone pillow, poured oil on it and said, 'This is God's house, how He gets in is up to Him.'

80. And it came to pass that Jacob met Rachel at the well; Jacob kissed Rachel and lifted up his voice and wept.

'Oh, kinky, eh,' said Rachel.

When Laban heard the tidings of Jacob, his sister's son, he ran to meet him, embraced and kissed him. 'Easy,' said Jacob, 'I'm straight.'

81. And Laban said to him, 'Surely, thou art my bone and flesh.'

'Sorry,' said Jacob, 'all my bone and flesh are mine.' And he abode in the house of Laban. Laban had two daughters: Leah, who was tender-eyed but, oh, Jacob saw that Rachel was beautiful and well-favoured, all over. And he, Jacob, had steam in his trousers. Through the steam and the throbbing Jacob spoke unto Laban, 'Can I have your daughter's hand?'

'You can have the rest as well,' sayeth Laban, 'but not until you serve me for seven years.'

And Jacob said, '*Seven* bloody years?'

82. For seven bloody years Jacob shovelled dung on Laban's fields and he reeketh so that no one would draweth nigh unto him. As he shovelled dung, he could see dear Rachel's face through it and he was comforted from the waist up.

83. And Jacob said unto Laban, 'My seven years are up.'

'I wondered what was up,' said Laban. 'I thought it was my blood pressure.'

So there was a wedding feast; before it was over Jacob grabbed Rachel and took her, saying, I feel a honeymoon coming on and was lost in the steam from his trousers. And through the night they begatted.

84. But woe, at dawn Jacob saw he had not been begatting Rachel, but Leah her sister. Jacob was cast down but eventually got up. 'Woe, who has done this to me?' he said.

'Nobody's done anything to you,' said Leah, 'you've been doing it to me; it was the will of my father that this happened.'

'Where is Rachel?' said Jacob.

'He was saving her for afters,' said Leah.

'Wherefore is my Rachel?' said Jacob.

85. Then Laban explained: 'It must not be done to give the younger before the elder. Fulfil her week.'

So Jacob fulfilled Leah's week. Then Laban brought Rachel and Jacob started to fulfil her. But Leah conceived Reuben, then she bore Simeon, then Levi, then Judah.

86. And though Jacob still fulfilled Rachel, she was

barren, so Rachel said, will you fulfil my maid, Bilhah —
so Bilhah bore a son and Rachel adopted him and said,
'I shall call him Dan.' While she was doing that Jacob
was doing it to the maid again and she had another boy
Naphtali — and the Lord said, 'Lo, a football team is
nigh.' Then Joseph did it with Leah's maid, Zilpah, and
she had a goalie named Gad, then she had a centre
forward named Asher, and now Jacob, who walked
with a zimmer, came out. Leah went out to meet him
and she saw that owing to his work he wore no trousers
and he said, 'I have hired thee with my son's mandrakes.'

87. 'I'm not for hire,' said Leah, 'I'm free.' And he
lay with her that night, but not for long: he soon
started to fulfil her, along came son No. 5 Issachar,
then No. 6 Zebulun; in between, Jacob slept in a
wheelchair, from it they lifted him on and off. Next he
fulfilled Rachel's mandrakes and had son Joseph.

88. And it came to pass that Jacob knocketh off
Laban's cattle, his mandrakes and took his wives and
football team with him. The Lord was angry and said,
'What are ye doing?'

And Jacob said, 'A bunk.' Whereupon Jacob putteth
black pepper on his camels' bums and they raced away
to the land of Coobel-ars.

89. But Laban rose up and, putting black pepper on
his camels' bums, goeth like the clappers. He caught up
Jacob by the Coobel-ars. Laban went in Jacob's tent,
then out of it into Leah's tent, then into the two
maidservants' tent; but he seeth them not, then he went

out of Leah's tent and into Rachel's tent, then out of that tent back into Jacob's tent. Then he seeth a camel with a hot bum and six legs and, lo, two of the legs were Jacob's.

'I knowest thou are behind there,' sayeth Laban.

'So do I,' said Jacob, stepping forth and showing his mandrakes.

'Are those my mandrakes?' sayeth Laban.

'Nay,' said Jacob, 'the camel ate yours.'

'Then open that camel,' said Laban in wrath.

90. 'Nay,' said Jacob, clutching his mandrakes. 'Yon camel is on a time lock.'

Then Laban cried out to heaven, 'Lord, why hast thou done this on me?'

And the Lord said, 'I haven't done anything on you.'

'It must have been the camel,' said Laban.

❀ CHAPTER IV ❀

AND IN TIME ALL THE SOULS that came out of the loins of Jacob were seventy souls. And Jacob died and his wives gave thanks for the rest. And, lo, the children of Israel went into Egypt where there was a higher rate of pay, better working conditions and BUPA. But Pharaoh saw how fast the children of Israel mutiplied — already all the gown shops were Jewish — so he enslaved them, made their lives bitter with hard bondage in mortar, in brick double glazing and pyramid aftersales, but still the children of Israel multiplied finding time to do it in the lunch break and, lo, the lunch breaks grew longer and longer. So Pharaoh sayeth all male babies would be thrown in the river. This would require a mighty throw as the river was a mile away.

2. The wife of Levi, thanks to a good lunch break, bore a son. 'Wrong!' said Levi. 'You know very well boys have got to be drowned.'

'I thought it was bank managers,' she said. That night the wife took the babe to the river and floated him away with some smoked salmon sandwiches.

'What are they for?' said Levi.

'He's a growing boy,' said the wife.

3. So the babe floated away on a compass bearing of Nor Nor East. It so happened that Pharaoh's daughter, there being no mains water at the palace, was having a bath in the river on a compass bearing of Nor Nor East, when floating by came the little basket.

4. 'Oh look,' said the princess, 'smoked salmon sandwiches. But wait! What's that next to them; it's a baby, what's he doing in there?' And she looked and he had done everything in there. 'This is one of the Hebrews' children; see, he's had a bit snicked off.'

And she called him Moses because that was his name. And he grew up as her son with an inside leg measurement of thirty-seven inches, and an area set aside for things. When the tailor asked which side he dressed, he said near the window.

5. When Moses had grown he went on a day trip to see the Hebrews building a temple and he saw their overseers beateth the shit out of them. He spied an Egyptian smiting a Hebrew, Wallop Thud Kerpow, so he slew the Egyptian and buried him in the sand. And the Lord said, 'Moses, what hast thou done?'

And he said, 'I done him.'

When Pharaoh heard this, he sought to slay Moses, but running like the clappers, Moses fled to a B&B area and a job centre.

6. And it came to pass that while reading *The Oldie* the Pharaoh died of boredom and the children of Israel gave a great sigh. God heard their groaning; it kept Him awake all night and He fitteth double glazing. Moses had a flexitime job looking after sheep.

7A. An angel of the Lord appeared to him in a burning bush.

'You all right in there?' said Moses.

God called unto him from the burning bush.

'How do you do that?' said Moses.

'It's better than Paul Daniels,' God said. 'Draw not nigh: for this land where thou standest is holy ground owned by the Church Commissioners.'

So Moses taketh off his shoes and God said, 'Verily, thou needest OdorEaters.'

7B. God went on a bit, then He said, 'I am come to deliver the children of Israel.'

'It'll take it out of you,' said Moses; 'they have about ten kids a week.'

'Nay, I am come,' said God, 'to take them into the land of milk and honey unto the place of Canaanites, Hittites, Amorites, Perizzites, Hivites and Jebusites, all good Jewish third-division teams.'

Moses went unto the children of Israel and said, 'I will lead you to a land of milk and honey.'

And they said, 'We won't last long on that, we need protein.'

8. And the Lord spake unto Moses and his footbath: 'Go to Pharaoh and say let my people go or I will smite all thy borders with frogs: the frogs shall come upon thee, verily, frogs will be everywhere, even in private parts.'

'It soundeth a bit kinky, but I shall do it,' said Moses. So he sayeth it all to the Pharaoh, who called for a psychiatrist's report. Moses stretched his hand over the waters and, lo, Egypt was covered with frogs and not a French chef in sight.

Then spoke the Pharaoh from under a hundred and sixty frogs, 'Moses, call them off and your people can go.'

So Moses sprinkled Dettol and the frogs goeth. Moses said unto the children of Israel, 'Our people can go.' Some went but some had already been.

9. And so the children of Israel left Egypt – many Egyptian bank managers committed suicide. And Moses said, 'The Lord sayeth for seven days thou shalt eat unleavened bread, thou shalt not eat leaven bread.'

'Are chips all right?' said the children of Israel.

The Lord said unto Moses, 'Every firstborn lamb thou shall redeem; if thou will not redeem it, break its neck.'

'How's that?' said Moses.

'When thy son asketh what is that, thou will say it's a lamb with a broken neck,' said the Lord.

'What about vegetarians?' said Moses.

'The same applies, only with a carrot,' said the Lord.

10. So Moses led the children of Israel into the desert. The Lord went before them by day in a pillar of cloud and by night in a pillar of fire. It was very distracting. Back in Egypt Pharaoh regretted letting the children of Israel go, there wasn't a decent tailor in town. He hardened his heart and arteries and, taking six hundred chariots and three aspirins, he set off in pursuit of them. The children of Israel were camping by the sea, then they saw the approaching Egyptians and

were sore afraid, some were sorer than others and had to use ointment.

11. Many burnt their bank statements. And Moses said unto the people, 'Fear not, for the Egyptians whom ye have seen today, ye shall see them again no more for ever.'

'Pardon???' said the children of Israel.

'Watch this,' said Moses and, using an east wind, he held his hand over the sea and, lo, the seas divided and the children of Israel escaped along the bottom.

'What did I tell you?' said Moses.

'Oh wow,' said the children of Israel.

But the Egyptians pursued them and Pharaoh shouted, 'Charge!'

And the Israelites were sore afraid, they did not like being charged for anything and they cried out to the Lord, 'Can't we settle out of court?'

12. And it came to pass that in the morning the Lord was on a pillar of fire and cloud, and when it cleared, he saw the Egyptians close upon the children of Israel. And the Lord said unto Moses, 'Stretch out thine hand over the sea.'

But Moses was sore afraid, 'Will it work a second time?' And, lo, it did. The waters returned, marked not known here, and drowneth the Egyptian Army and its chariots. Thus the Lord had saved Israel, who saw the Egyptians dead on the seashore. 'Oi vay,' said Moses, 'this will ruin the holiday trade.'

13. And the children of Israel journeyed into the desert, praising the Lord. And the Lord went before

them in a pillar of smoke whence cometh coughing. And Moses built an altar to the Lord. And the Lord said, 'Wherefore in the desert did ye find to build with?'

'It's Lego,' said Moses.

But woe a hunger came up the children of Israel and they cried out, 'All the chicken livers have gone – and so unto the gefilte fish.'

Moses said, 'Lord, help or they will be stoned.'

The Lord said, 'It won't be the first time you've been stoned.' And the Lord promised he would rain bread from heaven.

'Will it stay fresh that long?' said Moses. And in the morning there lay a small round thing. Moses said, 'Behold, this is the bread the Lord hath given.'

'That won't go far,' said the children of Israel.

'Wait,' said Moses, 'that's only for starters.'

14. As he spoke bread in bounty fell, striking Moses a glancing blow and injuring many. And they gathered bread, two omers for one man or one man for two omers; an omer is a tenth part of an ephah so those who had ephahs did well. Moses said, 'Thank you, Lord God, for the omers and ephahs; just tell us what it means.'

15. Then cometh a drought with hosepipe bans in Kent. 'Lord, we dieth of thirst,' said Moses.

'First it's bread, now it's water,' said the Lord, 'what next?'

'Money,' said Moses.

The Lord was wrath as he liketh not Jewish humour.

And he told Moses, 'Take a stick and take it to yon rock, smite it.' Moses took the stick, smote the rock and water squirteth out and the Israelites came to drink of it, and the Lord said, 'Drink ye not until thou hast boiled it.' But many heareth not and, woe, there were squitters in the land.

16. The Lord said: when the trumpet soundeth, all will come to the mountain. It came to pass, in the morning there was thunder and lightning, there was cloud, the forecast was for rain and the trumpet soundeth exceedingly loud. Many people complained and shouteth, 'Stop that bloody row.'

Moses spake and God answered in a different voice, 'A gottle of gear, a gottle gear.'

And Mount Sinai was on a smoke, because the Lord descended upon it in fire and smoke and the whole mountain quaked, and the children of Israel cried out, 'We are not insured against such things.'

Then the Lord said, 'Now hear this. Thou shalt not kill. Thou shalt not commit adultery.'

'It's a bit late for that, Lord,' said Moses. Then a flash of lightning and the Lord said, 'Thou shalt not steal.'

Oh dear, thought Moses, there goes the business.

Then the Lord, speaking through an anvil-topped nimbus, said, 'Thou shalt not bear false witness against thy neighbour.'

'But', said Moses, 'their bloody dog barks all night.'

Then there came around the Lord a burst of fire, and the children of Israel could hear Him trying to put it out. In between first-degree burns the Lord said, 'Thou shalt not covet thy neighbour's wife.'

CHAPTER IV

A great groan went up from the men of the Israelites.

And God spoke from a cloud of steam and He shed-deth six pounds. 'Ye will not make gods of silver nor make gods of gold.'

The children of Israel thanked the Lord, knowing the family cutlery and jewellery were safe.

The Lord went on: 'If thou wilt make me an altar of stone, be it not hewn stone: for if thou lift up thy tool upon it, thou hast polluted it.'

Never hence did Moses lift his tool upon it and they blessed him. It had been a close thing.

❧ CHAPTER V ❧

THE GLORY OF THE LORD ABODE ON MOUNT SINAI, which was Church property with a good lease. And the Lord called Moses from the midst of His latest cloud and Moses went into the midst of the cloud. 'Moses where art thou?' said the Lord.

'Mainly lost,' said Moses.

Moses was on the Mount forty days and forty nights, trying to find his way out.

The Lord charged Moses to make an ark: 'Thou shalt make bars of shittim wood, five for the boards of one side of the tabernacle, five bars for the boards of the other side of the tabernacle and five bars for the off side of the tabernacle, for the two sides westwards. And the middle bar in the midst of the boards shalt reach from end to end, and thou shalt overlay the boards with gold.'

'Not so fast, Lord,' said Moses, who was taking it down.

2. 'Make thou rings of gold,' continued the Lord, 'then there will be bars and thou shalt overlay the bars with gold. Thou shalt rear up the tabernacle according to the fashion thereof, and thou shalt make a veil of blue and purple and scarlet fine twined linen, of cun-

ning work with cherubims shalt it be made, and then four pillars of shittim wood. The hooks shall be of gold on four sockets of silver and thou shalt hang up the veil under the taches.'

'It's no good, God,' said Moses, 'we'll have to get a builder.'

In time, allowing for labour problems, an ark and tabernacle was made; it shone with gold and silver and the insurance on it was great.

3. The children of Israel carrieth the tabernacle to the appointed place, but it weighed mightily and, woe, there were ruptures and hernias. 'Moses,' said the Lord from behind a rock, 'thou shalt kill a ram, take his blood, put it on the tip of the right ear of your brother Aaron, then on the tips of the right ears of his sons, then upon the thumbs of the right hands, then upon the great toes of their right feet, then sprinkle on the knees.'

'Isn't this a bit silly, Lord?' said Moses.

The Lord went on and on, 'Take the blood and sprinkle on Aaron and his garments.'

'Those stains will never come out, Lord,' said Moses.

'Behold, I send an angel before thee. Provoke him not as he is a black belt and thou shalt make an altar of shittim wood and staves of shittim wood thou will make and overlay them with gold.'

'Wouldn't you rather see the natural wood?' said Moses and, lo, Moses and DIY made an altar of shittim wood.

4. When the people saw that Moses delayed to come down from the mountain, they said, 'This man who brought us from Egypt, what has become of him?'

And Aaron said, 'He's become a "schlepper".'* When Moses was gone the children of Israel fashioned a calf of gold.

And the Lord was wrath with them and from behind a fresh rock said, 'See the children of Israel, they are a stiff-necked people.'

'That's through sleeping in draughts,' said Moses.

5. And it came to pass, as Moses drew nigh unto the camp there he saw the golden calf and he saw nude dancing. Moses' anger waxed hot: about a hundred and ten degrees Fahrenheit. And he took the calf of gold, ground it to dust, poured it into the water and made the children of Israel drink it, thus increasing their value. And Moses saw the children of Israel were naked and of some of the men he was jealous.

'Who is on the Lord's side?'

'Never mind his side,' said the Israelites; 'get him off our back.'

Moses said whosoever will obey the Lord come across. Sons of Levi came across. 'It was time they came across,' said Moses. 'Take up thy sword, go, and any man that hath danced naked before the golden calf, smite his parts from the land even if he is begatting.'

'We will do thy bidding,' said the Levis, 'but it's not going to look good in the papers.' In the morning there came great wailing from the women as there was no insurance for smiting of parts.

6. Tuesday, early closing in Catford. And the Lord

* A lackey

spoke to Moses face to face: a nasty shock for both of them.

7. 'Observe,' said the Lord, 'I will drive out before thee the Amorites, the Canaanites and the Hittites.'

'There's no need to drive them out, let the bastards walk.'

And the Lord blessed Moses from a raincloud. 'Thrice in a year shall all your men appear before the God of Israel.'

'Any special dates?' said Moses.

'Yes,' said the Lord, 'any special dates.' And He blessed Moses from a thundercloud and got soaked to the skin.

And the Lord called Moses unto the mountain, and Moses trembled because the walk to the top of the mountain shaggeth him out. He was with the Lord forty days and forty nights, he ate not bread and drank not water, and he loseth weight and, lo, his trousers falleth down. The Lord liked not what he saw. ''Tis a small thing, but mine own,' said Moses.

8. And when Moses came down from the mountain the people saw that his face shone with a bright light and the people did hide their eyes, so Moses put a veil over his face and walketh into a brick wall. Whenever he speaketh to the Lord he taketh off the veil, and when he came back to the people, he putteth the veil back on and straightaway walked into a brick wall again. Then he placed the tabernacle in a tent of goat skin; on hot days it was unbearable, and Moses hideth his nose until it passeth. And by the door of the

tabernacle he placeth a burnt offering of meat and two veg.

The Lord put a great cloud over the tabernacle and Moses falleth over it.

9. And the Lord called for a burnt offering be it of fowls, pigeons or turtledoves, 'Wring off their heads'.

'Look, Lord, you're asking for trouble with the RSPCA and vegetarians.'

But the Lord feareth not as his solicitor was David Napley. The Lord spoke from behind a blancmange, 'Sprinkle thou the blood on the altar cloth.'

Moses groaned, 'Lord, you'll never get the stains out.'

'The blood of the sacrifice,' went on the Lord: 'thou shall dip thy finger in and touch four corners of the altar.'

'You still into all that?' said Moses.

And the Lord called the Israelites, 'Now hear this, then thou shall eat.'

'Lord, we're all in the middle of lunch,' said Moses.

The Lord heareth and said, 'Of these ye may eat the locust, the bald locust, the beetle, and the grasshopper.'

'Lord, we'll bloody well starve,' said Moses.

10. In time the Lord said unto the Israelites, 'When ye come unto the land of Canaan I will put a plague on a house of your possession.'

And Moses was cast down because it would lower the resale value.

The Lord spoke again, this time from out of a flour sack, 'If the plague continues, a priest will break down the house, all the stones and shittim wood be taken to a dump.'

Moses was cast down and said, 'Are you sure you're not Jeremy Beadle?' But when they came into Canaan there was no plague in the house and Moses taketh down the 'For Sale' sign and remortgaged in his wife's name.

11. The Lord spake unto Aaron [it was Moses' day off], 'When any man hath a running issue out of him he is unclean.' Aaron knew it was the dysentery.

'Everywhere he sitteth shall be unclean.'

'Yea – stains,' said Aaron.

The Lord went on: 'He that sitteth on anything *he* sitteth on shall be unclean and wash his clothes.'

'Water won't get it out,' sayeth Aaron, who himself was suffering; his family slept with all the windows open.

12. The Lord spoke more, 'And if any man's seed of copulation go out of him he shall be unclean until the even.'

'Fear not, Lord, genetic fingerprinting will find him,' said Aaron.

And the Lord blessed Aaron and his DNA. 'Thus,' said the Lord, 'separate the children of Israel from their uncleanness, that they die not in their uncleanness.'

And Aaron promised he would have a bath before he died.

And the Lord sayeth unto Aaron, 'Come into the holy place. Put on this holy vest and this linen coat, now these silken breeches, girdle thyself with linen, wear this hat.'

Aaron did the Lord's bidding and looked a real nana and he crieth out, 'Does anyone knowest a good tailor?'

And the Lord bade Aaron, 'Go unto my altar. Put incense on the fire.'

Aaron did so, a great cloud of incense covered the altar, in it Aaron could hear the Lord coughing.

13. The Lord spake unto Moses [he was back from lunch]: 'Tell the children of Israel I am the Lord God.'

And Moses turned to them and said, 'He is the Lord God.'

The Lord said, 'None of you shall approach any kin to uncover their nakedness. I am the Lord. The nakedness of thy father or mother thou shalt not uncover. I am the Lord. The nakedness of thy sister thou shalt not uncover. I am the Lord. Thou shalt not uncover the nakedness of thy father's sister. I am the Lord.'

'He keeps saying that,' said Moses.

And the Lord goeth on about nakedness, giving the children of Israel a good hour's listening. 'Listen,' said the Lord.

'Here He comes again,' said Moses.

'Thou shalt not lie with mankind, as with womankind.'

And a great wail went up from the gay Israelites.

'Neither shalt any woman stand before a beast to lie down thereto: it is confusion, it's also dangerous.'

14. The Lord spake from behind a waterfall and got soaked: 'Whoever giveth his seed to Molech I will cut off! If people hide their eyes when he giveth his seed to Molech I will kill not, I will set my face against those who commit whoredom with Molech.'

'Lord,' said Moses, 'I know not who Molech is, but he seems to be having all the fun.'

15. At one time Moses was bored of the day, and asked, 'Lord, you want anyone stoned today?'

The Lord said, 'Ye shall inherit the land.'

And Moses praised the Lord for he already had outline planning permission.

And the Lord spoke, 'Thou shall sanctify me, therefore I offer thee bread.'

'Any butter?' said Moses.

16. 'They shall not make baldness upon their head.' Moses pleaded for the balds but the Lord said, 'Nay, for on moonlit nights they shineth and give our position away.'

17. 'Neither shall thou shave off the corners of your beard.'

'No, no, Lord,' beseeched Moses, 'never cut corners.'

The Lord quieted Moses with a bolt of thunder: 'And ye shall take a wife in her virginity.'

'That'll take a lot of finding,' said Moses.

'A widow, a divorced woman, a profane woman or a harlot, this he will not take.'

'You're a bit late with that,' said Moses.

'Speak unto Aaron, saying, whoever hath a blemish, he will offer not the bread of his Lord.'

Moses was cast down for he knew Aaron and his sons had acne and boils.

'No bread shalt go to he who has anything superfluous.'

Moses wept, for the way things were *his* was superfluous.

18A. 'If a man hath a running issue he shalt eat not of holy things.'

Moses searched the camp, but saw no men running around with an issue.

The Lord worked in mysterious ways and that was another one of them.

'That which dieth shall not eat of my bread.'

Moses wondered did he hear right.

'Any man torn with beasts shall not eat the bread.'

Moses searched the camp looking for those torn by wild beasts, there were none save one bitten by doggie. The Lord spoke from behind a mound of potatoes. He said, 'No bread wilt thou give to offer to a blind man, a lame man, brokenfooted, brokenhanded, or he that hath a flat nose, a crookback, or scurvy or hath scabs or dwarf, with a wen.'

18B. 'Lord, that's just about all of us,' sayeth Moses.

The Lord said, 'Yea, and the Israelites will only eat holy things.'

'Lord,' said Moses, 'I've tried seven supermarkets and they don't have any: what's wrong with haddock?'

'I give up,' said the Lord. 'What's wrong with haddock?'

Moses bit his lip and clenched his fist.

'What ails my son?' said the Lord.

'I'm pissed off,' said Moses.

From behind a gasometer the Lord blessed Moses, and Moses bent low before the Lord; it got him in the back. With no holy things to eat the Israelites waxed angry. The Lord relented, but just to be on the safe side

He sent an angel down and He speaketh through him like a ventriloquist. 'Take thou a bullock that hath anything lacking in his parts.'

And Moses took the bullock, but none of his parts were missing. No, the bullock had bountiful parts. The angel said, 'Take thee the bullock and put him seven days under the dam.' And it came to pass, it drowned.

The Lord changed tack. 'Ahem! Take thou a ram with nothing superfluous.'

'The ram has a superfluous,' said Moses. 'But it's all his.'

18C. 'Use that for afters,' said the Lord. And they cooketh the ram, a burnt offering, some parts worse than others; twice Moses tried to offer it up to the Lord, but he couldn't reach. The angel of the Lord came down and took up a plate.

19. The Lord spake to Moses – they were still on speaking terms. 'Tell the children of Israel you shall reap the harvest, give it unto a priest and he will wave a sheaf, and on the morrow he will wave it again.' So for two days the priest waveth the sheaf and he getteth tennis elbow. And the Lord spoke, 'Thou shall make a meat offering. There shall be two-tenths deals of fine flour mingled with oil, one small onion, two cloves, one small bunch of parsley, 1 oz pepper, and a tablespoon lemon juice. Put in oven for twenty-five minutes. Sufficient for six persons.'

So they cooketh as the Lord instructed. They did eat of it and it was bloody awful.

And the Lord blessed them. He told the children of

Israel the fifteenth day shall be a feast of the tabernacles. 'For seven days there shall be no servile work.' But the Pakistanis heareth Him not. 'Ye shall dwell in booths seven days . . . I made the children of Israel to dwell in booths.'

So they all crammed into booths, but had to come out when somebody wanted to use the phone. The children of Israel liked not living standing up in a booth and, lo, claustrophobia came on the land and final demand phone bills.

20. The Lord was still on about food. He spoke from a thunderstorm and was badly singed.

'The Lord's eyebrows have gone,' Moses told the people. 'If only He'd stay in one place.'

And the Lord sayeth: 'Without the vail of the testimony, in the tabernacle of the congregation, shall Aaron order it from the evening unto the morning before the Lord continually.'

'You'll have to be clearer than that, Lord,' said Moses.

21. And it came to pass that the son of an Israelitish blasphemed the name of the Lord. 'He's a twit,' said the son; 'a great big twit.'

And they brought him unto Moses. 'You're a twit too,' said the son, and spat in Moses' eye, so they putteth the son in a ward where he claimeth to be the king of China. Then Moses, who observeth him through a key, knew the boy was not right.

'He is of the devil,' said the Lord. 'For his sins he must be banished.' So they banished him to Milton Keynes.

22. 'Lord,' said Moses, 'tell us of your new laws.'

CHAPTER V

And the Lord speaketh, 'If any man cause a blemish in his neighbour he shall giveth him his anti-blemish cream; and if he killeth a beast he shall restore it.'

'What, mouth to mouth?' said Moses.

'An eye for an eye, a tooth for a tooth; that includes dentures,' said the Lord. 'And on the last Sunday of the month, at dawn the trumpet will blow throughout the land.'

'That's a bit early, Lord,' said Moses; 'we usually have a lie-in on Sunday.'

'In the year of the jubilee,' said the Lord, 'ye shall return every man unto his possessions.'

'Oi vay,' said Moses, 'that means I'll have to give the hallstand back to the Cohens.'

'Thou shall gather the fruits of the field and thou shall increase the price.'

'But Lord, I got a sale on, even at three shekels a kilo they're not selling.'

And the Lord blessed Moses; he was like that. Now the Lord spoke from his original Cloud I. 'The land shall not be sold for ever for the land is mine, ye are strangers and sojourners with me.'

Moses fell down and beat his breast, all this time and he knew not that God was his landlord.

23. 'And in all the land of your possession ye shall grant a redemption for the land.'

Moses rent his garments for his mortgage had but a month to go.

The Lord said, 'If thy brother was waxen poor, and fall into decay, thou shall relieve him.'

43

And Moses cried out, 'But, Lord, he already owes me money.'

'And thou will make free and welcome him into your house.'

It was war to Moses. 'Lord, we've only one spare room and the mother-in-law is in that.'

And the Lord spoke from behind Sainsbury's cheese counter: 'Ye that farm shall eat all your bread to the full.'

Moses ate all his bread and felt full and sick.

'I will give peace in the land and ye shall lie down.'

'Lie down?' said Moses. 'How are we going to get around?'

The Lord spake, 'For I will have respect unto you and multiply you.'

'Multiply me?' said Moses. 'How many Moses do you want?'

The Lord went on to say, 'And I will walk among you, and will be your Lord. It will be a *Daily Mirror* exclusive. If thou obeyest not my laws I will smite the children of Israel with consumption, burning ague.'

'But, Lord,' said Moses, 'we have no NHS, we'll have to go private. My father's operation for piles cost a fortune.'

24. The Lord said, 'If ye walk contrary unto me, I will bring seven plagues among you. If ye be not reformed by these things, and walk contrary unto me, then I will punish you seven times and if you harm not to me and still walk contrary to me, then so I will walk contrary unto you.'

'Oi vay,' said Moses, 'all this for not walking.'

❧ CHAPTER VI ❧

AND THE LORD NUMBERED THE CHILDREN OF ISRAEL and there were forty thousand and five hundred and they calleth out for proportional representation. The Lord asked the priests to estimate the people and they said a male from twenty unto sixty years, fifty shekels. Moses asked of them and they said seven shekels or near offer. And when a man shall sanctify his home then the priest shall estimate it whether it be good or bad. And, lo, Moses taketh down his 'For Sale' sign. And the Lord spake unto Moses, 'Number the children of Levi; from a month old and upward shalt thou number them.'

Using a Biro, Moses numbered them up to twenty pounds.

2. Then the Lord said, 'Moses, Aaron and his sons shall wait on their priest's office: and the stranger that cometh in the night shall be put to death.'

'Poor sod,' said Moses. And Moses took the redemption money of those who were over and above at the NatWest. Of the firstborn of Israel he took a thousand, three hundred and threescore and five shekels. And Moses cried as he handed all the money to Aaron, except a call-out charge.

3. And it came to pass that the children of Simeon

did make an offer to the tabernacle of one silver charger, value one hundred and thirty shekels, one silver bowl, thirty shekels, one golden spoon of ten shekels. Moses beat his breast for only the day before he had seen them all in Cohen's pawn shop. And they brought for sacrifice one bullock, one ram, one lamb, one goat, two oxen and a partridge in a pear tree. Before they slew the animals they had to wait for a Beth Din Rabbi. Next, for reasons only known to himself, the Lord said, 'Take the Levites, and cleanse them. Let them wash their clothes and let them shave all their flesh.' And, lo, there came about six hundred bald heads.

'Now what, Lord?' said Moses.

'Hear the voice of the children of Israel.'

And they crieth out, 'Wigs – give us wigs!'

The Lord spake, 'Bring the Levites forward, and the children of Israel shall put their hands upon them.'

But the children of Israel pulleth back, saying, 'We don't want to catch it.'

The Lord sayeth, 'Lo! The Levites will serve the tabernacle unto their fiftieth year of voluntary redundancy.'

4A. The Lord spoke unto Moses: 'And there were certain men who were defiled by the dead body of a man.'

'Fear not, Lord,' said Moses. 'We bury all our stiffs.'

The Lord sayeth, 'No man shall tarry with a dead body.'

And Moses said, 'I've only got my body; it's not dead yet but I have to tarry with it.'

'Now,' sayeth the Lord, 'on the fourteenth day thou shall eat unleavened bread, they shall none of it nor break any bone of it.'

'Bones?' said Moses. 'Bones in bread, Lord?' And it came to pass that Moses changed his baker.

4B. On the day of the passover the tabernacle reared up and a cloud appeared over the tabernacle and it deluged with rain.

'Lord,' said Moses, 'do we have to have this rain-cloud?'

'Yes,' said the Lord, 'there's a hosepipe ban on.'

By night the tabernacle had the appearance of being on fire, but this was done with cunning strobe lighting by the special effects department. Wherever the tabernacle journeyeth, the cloud goeth as well bringing torrential rain and flooding. The children of Israel cried out in misery. The Lord asked what ailed them, and Moses said, 'They are pissed off with the weather, Lord.'

The Lord spoke unto Moses, 'Make thee two trumpets of silver.'

'Can't we use brass?' said Moses. 'We're a bit short of money.'

The Lord heareth him not. 'Thou may blowest them for assembly in the camp.'

'Sort of Butlins?' said Moses.

'When ye blow the alarm, then the camps that lie on the east side shall go forward. When ye blow a second alarm, the camps that lie on the west side will go forward.' So it came that when the trumpet sounded both sides collideth.

4C. The Lord spoke to Moses: 'In the beginning of your month, ye shall blow with the trumpets over your burnt offerings.'

'Lord,' said Moses, 'why do we have to eat burnt food; for once can't we grill it?' And when the Israelites complained the Lord God couldn't take it, the fire of the Lord came amongst them.

'Lord, Lord,' crieth out Moses, 'what are you doing?'

'I'm sorry,' said the Lord. 'I don't know what came over me.'

'Look, Lord,' said Moses, 'we aren't insured against arson.' And the Lord quencheth the flames and Moses called in the assessors.

5. Then there was a hunger on the land. The people called out, 'Who shall give us flesh to eat?'

Lo, it was not safe for plump people to walk abroad at night. 'We remember the fish,' they said, 'which we ate in Egypt.' Moses remembered it too, it was a Nile perch and weighed six pounds; he also remembered the new potatoes and the onions, with brown gravy. Ah yes, and a bottle of Château Latour.

6. And Miriam and Aaron spoke against Moses for he had married an Ethiopian. 'She's a schwartzer,' said Mirian. 'Yes, and me with a daughter just ready for a shidduck!'

7. And the Lord came down in a pillar of cloud sneezing, sneezing, sneezing and He said to Miriam and Aaron, 'Though Moses hath married a schwartzer, thou shall not see her in a bad light.'

'She's the same colour in any light,' said Miriam.

The Lord was wrath. 'She is of the same flesh and blood as ours.'

'Yes, but it's a different colour,' said Miriam. 'He's married out of the faith; wait till his mother hears about this.'

With that the pillar of cloud departed and, behold, Miriam became leprous.

And Moses, from a safe distance, cried out to the Lord. 'Heal her now, O God, I beseech thee.' And Moses prostrated himself. And lo, Miriam's leprosy was cured. 'Verily,' said Moses, 'it's amazing what a little grovelling will do.'

And Miriam in her joy danceth naked before the tabernacle. And, lo, Moses saw that she had big ones, and he praised the Lord for both of them.

8. The Lord spoke unto Moses, 'Send thou men that will search the land of Canaan, not industrial but suburban.' So Moses sent Joshua and a surveyor and they returned after forty days and nights [why always forty, thought Moses] and told him the land floweth with milk and honey.

'We've had all that before,' said Moses, 'but it's not enough.'

They went on, 'But the tribes are strong, the cities are walled and have a neighbourhood watch . . . It is a land that catch up the inhabitants, the men are like giants, we were like grasshoppers before them, so we hopped it.'

'Very funny,' said Moses.

9. So terrible was the joke that all the congregation

lifted up their voice and called, 'Bring back Benny Hill', and Caleb cried, 'We were all better off in Egypt.'

Moses and Aaron fell on their faces, both breaking their noses and smashing teeth.

'Upsydaisy,' sayeth the Lord.

The children of Israel were displeased with Moses and Aaron and started to stone them and they runneth like fuck to safety.

And the Lord appeared in the steam from the laundry: 'Moses, whyfore are the people in bad humour after all my signs of goodwill?'

Moses said, 'The council made us take the signs down as unsightly. We're in a conservation area.'

The Lord said, 'Then the Israelites sinneth, I will punish them according to your word.'

'What word was that, Lord?' said Moses.

'No credit given here,' said the Lord. Yea, the Lord was long suffering; doctors said it was lumbago. He said unto Moses, 'You and your people shall wander in the wilderness forty years.'

When Moses told the children of Israel this, they stoneth him again. For the second time he runneth like fuck for cover.

The Lord said, 'Why do the people turn away from me?'

The children of Israel spoke as one, which took a lot of rehearsing and said, 'Lord, thou art suffering over-exposure.'

10. And while the children of Israel were in the wilderness they found a man that had gathered sticks

on the Sabbath day, and they brought him to Moses who put him in a ward, not on the NHS but privately, for they knew not what should be done with him.

And the Lord said, 'The man must be surely put to death, the congregation shall stone him.'

And the children of Israel gathered for a good day's stoning, but the man sayeth, 'I want to see a solicitor.'

When he did there was a call-out fee; the solicitor sayeth, 'He who is without sin cast the first stone.' A wave of disappointment came from the crowd.

The Lord spake unto Moses from behind a waterfall and collided with a rock. 'Moses, your children shall wander in the wilderness forty years, and bear your whoredoms, until your carcases be worn and wasted.'

'Oh no, Lord, they don't do it that much, some only do it part-time; in the day they do aromamassage.'

11. But it came the children of Israel repented of their ways, and they rose up early and got them up the mountain saying, 'Lo, this is bloody hard going.'

The Lord spoke from behind a wall, but the acoustics were so woeful, he had to pull a brick out and speak through that. 'Thou must maketh an offering to the Lord; one offering will be of meat, medium-rare, with chips; and a second offering of wine, preferably a Château Latour 31 BC.'

12. As they wandered in the wilderness some looked for lost golf balls, and the Lord went before them by daytime in a pillar of cloud and in a pillar of fire at night; sometimes, during heavy rain, the pillar of fire went out and had to be relit. One day there camest

Korah with two hundred and fifty of his soldiers and sayeth to Moses, 'You promised a land of milk and honey, all we get is a wilderness. We want our mortgage money back.'

Moses fell on his face and he cometh up without teeth, and the Lord saw and was wrath. 'Hear this, they that believeth not, the earth will open her mouth and down you'll go.'

And, lo, the earth opened and Korah was swallowed up.

Moses saw and was in awe. 'Jesus Christ,' he said.

The Lord said, 'Hey, that will be a good name for my son. Now watch this.' And there came out a great fire that consumed two hundred and fifty of Korah's men.

'Lord, how did you do that?'

The Lord said, 'Just like that.'

'Well, I wouldn't like that,' said Moses. But the people were blaming Moses for the death of Korah and his men. He saw the people gathering stones and woe he had the shits; he crieth out to the Lord, the Lord knew it was too late as Moses had already done it. It came to pass, the people gathered at the tabernacle.

And the Lord spake unto Moses: 'Flee this congregation ere I consume it with fire.'

13. Moses was fearful, there was no insurance cover against fire. He told Aaron, 'Quick, take incense among the congregation; the Lord is wrath; the plague is begun.' Aaron runneth like the clappers among the congregation with incense; all around the Israelites were snuffing it. Moses stood between the living and the dead.

'Which are you?' said Aaron.

And the congregation cried out, 'We don't want incense, we need a doctor.'

And, behold, the plague ceased. 'Just like that,' said the Lord. Fourteen thousand had been killed by the plague.

'It's no way to make friends, Lord,' said Moses.

The Lord told Moses, 'Take ye twelve princes of Israel, maketh them to write their names on a rod, then lay them on the tabernacle.' And Moses doeth. After dark he laid the rods on the altar, and reflected they weren't the only things being laid that night. After a hard night at the Ethiopian, Moses saw of all the rods the one with Aaron's name on had bloomed blossoms, for he had used rooting powder.

14. And the Lord said, 'Aaron, thou shall keep thy charge and the charge of all the tabernacles.'

Aaron said, 'But Lord, I'm not smoking that stuff any more.'

The Lord said, 'Thou shall offer a meat dish Steak Diane, well done with boiled potatoes and peas, and all the males shall eat thereof. The meal is your heave offering, and this heave shall be unto you.'

So Aaron got Moses to heave the dinner at him. 'Now what, Lord?' said Aaron.

'The dry cleaners,' sayeth the Lord.

15. It came to pass that Miriam died and Moses mourned because when he had a confrontation with his Ethiopian woman he would seek comfort with Miriam who laid hands on him. Still, there was always Rebecca

with her aromamassage. The Lord appeared and He told Moses, 'I am wrath with Aaron. Take him up unto the Mount and strip him.' So Moses stripped Aaron and, lo, he was naked; many women applauded because he hath noble proportions. Moses put Aaron's clothes on his son, who, screaming, runneth to the nearest tailor.

16. Aaron dieth of indecent exposure, and his wife Meribah casheth in his policy and goeth on the piss. The Lord was wrath but it didn't stop her. For Aaron they mourned for thirty days. Moses sayeth, 'Aaron is no longer with us; in fact, he's not with anyone.' And woe there was a drought on the land, the fields were cracked and parched.

17. Many Israelites were cracked and parched and they had a wrath against Moses. He was sore afraid because he saw the children gathering stones. He runneth like hell to a rock, which he smote, but no water came; he smote it again and again.

'You're using the wrong end,' sayeth the Lord. The first stones were bouncing off his head; turning the stick around he smote and rock and water gushed forth. Next was the famine and the people cried out, 'There beeth no bread; and our soul loatheth this light bread. We want brown wholemeal with the flavour locked in.' And for reasons beyond comprehension, the Lord hurled down fiery serpents that fell flaming among the Israelites' tents. They asked Moses what he was doing to help and he said, 'I'm praying for you.'

'That's no bloody good,' said the Israelites, 'we want the fire brigade and snakebite antidote.'

CHAPTER VI

The Lord said unto Moses, 'Make thou a brass serpent, set it on a pole.'

And he doeth it – and all those sick with snakebite did live. 'But Lord, what about the fire damage?'

'I'm sorry about that,' said the Lord.

Moses said, 'You're sorry.'

Lo! The Lord said, 'Gather the people together, and I will give them water.'

18. 'Lord,' said Moses, 'what about the stick and the rock?'

'It's empty,' sayeth the Lord. 'It only held five hundred gallons.' Came a day when the Israelites, due to mortgage repossessions, moved on to Mattanah, from there to Nahaliel to Bamoth to Lewisham to Moab to Catford to Pisgah to Jeshimon. Now all the tents were B&B (Breakfast and Bugger-off).

19A. The Israelites set forward and pitched on the plains of Moab. And Moses chanted, 'Woe to thee, Moab! Thou art undone and we can see it all. Whose land is this?'

And a voice said 'Balak's.'

And Moses said, 'And Balaks to you.'

19B. The people of Moab were sore afraid and sayeth, 'These people that cometh from Egypt, they cover the face of the earth: that's why we can't see it.' Then Balaam, their king, went to see a solicitor to evict the Israelites. He saddled his ass and went. The ass saw the angel of the Lord standing in the way and the ass went in a field. Balaam did it against a tree; remounting, Balaam hit his ass. Again the angel stood in the way.

This time the ass thrust herself against a wall crushing Balaam down one side. Balaam hit her, then the ass collapsed with Balaam underneath and he smote the ass. The Lord opened the mouth of the ass: 'Why belteth me so, why belt thine own ass?'

20. Then the Lord appeared, 'Hast thou not heard of the RSPCA?' Balaam was sore afraid, and had a sore ass and Balaam whined. 'I have sinned for I know not that thou stoodeth in the way against me, now therefore if it displease thee I will get me back again.'

'You grovelling little creep, get you and your ass out of here,' said the angel.

21. And still one jump ahead of the bailiffs, the Israelites abode in Shittim. It was everywhere. And with the hot weather their men began to commit whoredom with the daughters of Moab. Lo, many were stricken with crabs. When Balaam returneth, he told Balak, 'I must say unto thee words the Lord putteth in my mouth.'

Balak said, 'Say Ahhh.'

Balaam sayeth Ah.

'I see no words inside,' said Balak.

'Oh dear, they must have fallen out,' said Balaam.

And they searched the ground for the words, and, lo, they found them and they sayeth, 'Final Demand: Rent.'

'The Lord is my shepherd,' said Balaam. 'He also beeth my landlord.'

And the Lord spoke of Inheritance Tax. 'If a man die and have no son, his inheritance will pass to his daughter, if he have no daughter, jolly hard luck.'

22. Moses bowed before the Lord but first he took painkillers.

The Lord said, 'Take thee Joshua and before all the congregation give him a charge.'

Moses gave him some charge and he smoketh it and said, 'Wow, daddy, the Lord is my shepherd, I'm tellin' you baby I shall not want, right on man, He maketh me to lie down in green, purple and yellow pastures.' Whereupon he zonketh out. And, lo, without a stone thrown, Joshua was stoned.

The Lord said unto Moses, 'Heal him.'

So Moses throweth a bucket of water over Joshua. The Lord blessed Moses, but only lightly.

23. The Lord sayeth, 'The first day of the month shall be holy, thou shall do no work.'

The children of Israel giveth three cheers. Moses was down, for that day he was to wallpaper the lounge.

The Lord spoke of a feast. 'Moses, thou shall sacrifice nine bullocks.'

'Bullocks?' said Moses.

'Bullocks,' said the Lord.

'Two rams and fourteen lambs.'

'Oh Lord,' said Moses, 'we'll never get them all in the oven.'

'Then', said the Lord, 'go thou to the land of the Aga and make a continual burnt offering.'

'Look, Lord,' said Moses, 'won't you settle for an omelette?'

The Lord waxed wrath and striketh Moses lightly with a thunderbolt of lightning, dissolving his socks. It taketh a week for Moses and his wife to chop up nine bullocks, rams and lambs, and the children of Israel came from near and far to partake of the Lord's feast and they all praised him save those with hiatus-hernia and wind, of which much was let go, and they had to raise the tent flaps.

24. And the Lord spoke unto Moses: 'Arm the children of Israel against the Midianites.' So they slew all the males, took all the women and their little ones and then burnt all the castles with fire; what a lot of bastards. And Moses was wrath. 'Kill all the males of the little ones and kill all women that hath lain with a man.' Verily, Moses was a bit of a bastard too. Now there were captured treasures, sixteen thousand seven hundred and fifty shekels, which Moses taketh and he placed it all on the tabernacle and offered it to the Lord until nightfall when he offered it into his mattress.

25. And the children of Gad spoke unto Moses: 'Ataroth, and Dibon, and Jazer, and Nimrah, and Heshbon, and Elealeh, and Shebam, and Nebo, and Beon.'

Moses knoweth not what they were talking about. 'Are they football teams?' he said.

'Nay, they have great cattle lands that we work.'

And Moses said, 'Well, it's agricultural land and it's six hundred shekels an acre and you must not use pesticides.'

The children of Gad moaned and clutched their wallets, beat their breasts, rent their garments, gnashed their teeth, tore their hair. By the time they finished they were in a pretty bad way. Moses settled for a cheque for four hundred and for four hundred in cash.

26. Then Moses said unto the Gads, 'What about the war with the Amonites? Shall your brethren fight while you sit here?' The children of Gad rose and said, 'We are conscientious objectors.'

And, lo, Moses was stymied but on only one leg. 'Go thou and build thy cities for your little ones, so go thou to McAlpines and Mowlems, then journey thou to the land of the Halifax. Take thou from them a mortgage.'

27. One day Aaron went up into Mount Hor as commanded by the Lord. He got to the top and cried, 'I'm here, Lord', and snuffed it. The police were called. There were no suspicious circumstances, just that one hundred and twenty-three-year-old men shouldn't climb mountains. The postmortem sayeth he dieth from a stroke; a stroke of luck for his wife who inheriteth his fortune.

28. The Lord said unto Moses, 'Tell the children of Israel they will cross the Jordan.'

And Moses said, 'Why not? They've crossed everybody else.'

Then said the Lord, 'They shall kill all the inhabitants, destroy all their pictures, their molten images and pluck down all their high places.'

Moses was wrath. 'You've only just done over the Amorites, now this!'

The Lord warneth, 'Unless thou killest them all, those that remain will be pricks in your eyes and thorn in your sides.'

Moses didn't want a prick in his eye so he telleth the Israelites to attack. It was a full-frontal attack; you could see everything. And until all the enemy were killed, many Israelites had a prick in their eyes.

29. And so the children of Israel came into the land of Jordan and the Lord said unto Moses, 'This land is for the people at reasonable rents. Now every man that killeth any persons unawares may flee thither.'

'Where is thither?' said Moses.

'Broadmoor,' said the Lord.

30. Now the Lord spoke from out of a skip. 'Ye shall not pollute the land whereon ye are.' Moses spoke not, but he knew many of the Israelites were doing it in the river. The Lord said, 'Blood defileth the land and cannot be cleansed.'

Moses sayeth, 'It doth cometh off with Flash.'

The Lord blessed Moses but wished he wouldn't keep interrupting.

31. The Lord said unto Zelophehad, 'Let thy daughters marry whom they wish, preferably a Doctor, Solicitor or an Accountant.' Zelophehad thanked the Lord with a post-dated cheque.

✃ CHAPTER VII ✃

AND IT CAME TO PASS, Moses spoke unto the children of Israel. It was the fortieth year of their time in the wilderness. And Moses said, 'Remember when the Lord spake unto us, "Behold, I have set the land before thee, go in and possess the land." And you went forth and possessed the land, taking down the "For Sale" signs as you did.'

Moses said, 'The Lord hath multiplied you as the stars of heaven, go now and multiply.'

'Multiply? Again?' said the children of Israel. 'You must be mad, half of us are at the bottom of the council housing list.'

And Moses said, 'How can I myself alone bear your cumbrance, and your burden, and your strife?'

'Get a secretary,' they said.

Moses beat his breast and said, 'My life.' He spoke on: 'Remember when we went through that great and terrible wilderness?'

The Israelites said, 'Yes, we would never have booked our holidays there had we known.'

2. 'Remember how in the wilderness the Lord bore thee, as a man doth bear a son?' And Moses recalled he and his wife couldn't bear their son. 'And ye are come

to the land of the Amorites and the Lord God doth give it to you.'

'But', cried the children of Israel, 'it was only leasehold.'

'And you were fearful of taking the land of the Amorites and cried out, "Lord, the Amorites are taller and bigger than us," and the Lord replied, "That is because they are on cod liver oil and malt and Sanatogen." And the Lord went before us and looketh for new land for the children of Israel P L C to settle. And the Lord said, "Ye are to pass through the coast of the children of Esau. Meddle not with them." And the Lord spake unto me, "Ye shall buy meat of them for money."'

'Oi vay money,' cried the Israelites. 'Hadn't we suffered enough?' And Moses said, 'And the Lord spake, "Ye shall also buy water of them for money."'

'Oh,' cried the Israelites, 'money for water! We can make money for nothing.'

And in time Moses said, 'Rise ye up.'

It took a while to get them all up.

Moses continued, 'And the Lord said unto me, "Now, pass over the River Arnon, I give unto you the king of the Amorites, and his land: begin to possess it. This day I put the dread of thee and the fear of thee amongst all nations."

'"Lord," I said unto him, "you are doing a great PR job."

'The Lord said, "Thou shall pass through the land of the Heshbon."'

CHAPTER VII

'Any properties going?' said the children of Israel.

'In that land you will buy meat for money.'

In a flash all the male Israelites formed a circle round their money crying, 'Nobody eats tonight.'

The Lord was wrath: verily, he was pissed off with the Israelites.

The Lord charged the children to possess the land of the Sihon, then Gillead, then Ammon, then Tabhok.

'Be careful, Lord,' said the children of Israel, 'we're becoming a monopoly!'

3. And it came to pass, Moses called all Israel again and said, 'You will put up no graven images nor the likeness of male or female nor any beast or any winged fowl nor anything that creepeth on the ground or any fish in the waters.'

And the children of Israel said, 'Can't we put up the wedding photographs?'

Moses spoke: 'Behold, the Lord, ye have heard the Lord speak to you from the midst of the fire.'

'But', said the Israelites, 'it's so hot we couldn't get near enough to hear what He was saying.'

The Lord called out, 'Get into your tents.'

4. They went into their tents and said, 'Now what?'

God said, 'I will speak unto thee all the commandments.'

'But Lord,' said the Israelites, 'we already know that, we've got them down on two stone tablets.'

'Hear me,' said the Lord, 'you will walk in the ways of the Lord, you will not turn left or turn right.'

'How are we going to turn round corners?' said the Israelites.

God said unto Moses, 'Thou shall teach the children, and they shall be as frontlets between thy eyes.'

'Quick,' said Moses to the people, 'look up what frontlets are because whatever they are I'm going to get it right between the eyes.'

The Lord said, 'Thou shall say unto thy son, we were Pharaoh's bondmen and I brought you out with a mighty hand.'

5. Moses gritted his teeth. 'But had we known this from the youngest to the oldest?'

'Yes,' said the Lord, 'it was by way of a repeat, and thou will smite the Hittites, the Girgashites, the Amorites, the Canaanites, I shall deliver them unto you.'

Surely that morning, six vans were delivered with the tribes and so the Israelites smote them and they were hard-pressed. 'Lord, I fear we are losing; do some of your tricks, please.'

6. And the Lord sent angels with fiery swords, and the enemies withdrew and surrendered. 'I am the Lord that freed you from Egypt.'

'Another repeat,' said Moses.

7. The Lord said, 'Thou shall not eat of them that chew the cud or them that divide the cloven hoof.'

'Lord,' said Moses, 'that only leaves rabbits.'

8. 'Then thou shalt turn it into money, hold thy money in thy hand, go unto a place which the Lord thy God shall choose, the mattress.' The Lord said, 'But of all clean fowl ye may eat — but of that that dieth of itself: thou shall give it to the stranger at the gate that

he will eat it and snuff it.' The Lord said, 'Remember, I am the God that tookest thee from Egypt.'

And Moses said, 'Lord, they're fed up hearing it.'

The Lord appeared in a raincloud and was drenched. 'Thou shall surely smite the inhabitants of the city, destroying it utterly and thou shall gather all the spoil and stuff thy mattresses.'

Moses, 'Sayeth, Lord, don't you think you are over-doing it? Wait until you get the bill for damages.'

The Lord said, 'Does thou trust me? I got you out of Egypt, remember.'

'Remember it? You never stop,' said Moses.

'Beware false prophets, thou must kill him, thou must be the first hand that shall stone him.'

'Lord,' said Moses, 'the town is full of stoned proph-ets and the dustmen won't take them away.'

'Fear not, they shall come to pass,' said the Lord.

'You're right, Lord, these dustmen go right past.'

The Lord spoke. 'The holy things thou hast thou shall take unto a place the Lord will choose, Milton Keynes.' And He said thy children will write the names of the chosen on the gateposts and they wrote Duran Duran, Elton John, Prince, Eric Clapton, Dick Strangle.

9A. From in the Jordan the Lord spoke; there were bubbles everywhere. 'Ye are the children, ye shall not cut yourselves, nor make any baldness between your eyes for the dead.'

And the children of Israel spoke: 'What's He talking about?'

'You are a crowd of ignoramuses,' said the angel of

the Lord. 'The Lord wills you to have plenty and turn it into money and put it in a safe place.'

'The mattress,' cried out the Israelites.

'And the poor man thou will help sufficient for his need in that which he wanteth, a Porsche. And thou shalt roast and eat in a place the Lord has chosen. Blooms. Also, thou shalt make an aul, and thrust it through his ear unto the door, and he shall be thy servant for ever.'

'Lord,' said the people, 'we don't want a servant hanging up by his ear on a door.'

The Lord said, 'At the end of seven years thou shall make a release.'

So Moses released his accountant because he was bloody awful.

9B. 'Hear me,' sayeth the Lord, 'thou shall not respect persons, neither take a gift: for a gift doth blind the eyes.'

The children of Israel said, 'Ye make it hard to give people presents.'

The Lord said, 'If there be found among you, men and women that had done wickedness in the sight of the Lord, they shall be cursed.'

'What happens to those you don't see?' said the Israelites.

'They will be remanded into custody,' said the Lord. 'And,' said the Lord, 'he that will not hearken to the Lord he shall die.'

'How?' sayeth the Israelites.

And the Lord said, 'You just have to wait.' After a

lie-down the Lord continued: 'The time will come when I will set a king over thee.'

'What about a queen?' said the Israelites.

10. The Lord said, 'The priests of the tribe shall eat the offering of the Lord made by fire grilled lightly with a side salad with prunes and custard.' And the Lord spoke of the king. 'Yea, when he comes, he shall not multiply horses to himself, nor cause the people to return to Egypt, to the end that he should multiply horses.'

'What are you talking about?' said the Israelites.

'Neither', went on the Lord, 'shall the king multiply his wives.'

'He must rest between each,' said the Israelites, 'that way he can see to the lot.'

11. The Lord said the priests shall eat the offering of the Lord made by fire, in this case sausage and mash, and there will be his inheritance, which are the fish knives and the parrot. Otherwise he will own nothing like the names at Lloyds.

'Amen,' said the Israelites.

'To the priest,' said the Lord, 'thou shall give to the priest an ox or a sheep, but only the best cuts, the first of thy corn, thy best wine, thine best oil, the first fleece of thy best sheep.'

And the children of Israel said, 'Lord, we'll have bugger-all left.'

The Lord was wrath. 'Do you want to go to arbitration?'

There beath no comeback as the Israelites were sore afraid and their solicitor was on holiday.

The Lord said, 'Behold, the priest shall also eat food that cometh from the sale of his patrimony, which is a two-bedroom flat, £8,000 ono.'

A low moan ariseth from the priest; he prostrateth himself at the altar and said, '£8,000 it's a giveaway.'

12. The Lord said, 'There shall not be found among you any one that maketh his son or daughter pass through the fire.'

'Lord,' said the Israelites, 'we could make anyone pass through the fire; it goes up the chimney.'

The Lord said, 'There shall be no wizards, witches, TV show host, an enchanter or a necromancer; these are abominations the Lord God will drive them out – they are all on the 9.20 to Glasgow.'

13. 'Thou shalt be perfect with the Lord thy God.'

'We are perfect with you, Lord,' said the children of Israel; 'it's the bloody neighbours.'

The Lord said, 'I will give unto thee a prophet.'

'We could do with a profit,' said the Israelites.

He bade them divide the land and submit plans to the Borough Council to build three cities; one city will be for wrongdoers, like a man who maketh a living pulling short measure beer. He can flee to a city called Birmingham where he will never be found. Two more cities they built: King's Cross. And the Lord spoke of the law. 'A life for a life, eye for an eye, tooth for a tooth, a piano for a piano, a deepfreeze for a deepfreeze, and a foot for a foot. Innocent blood must not be spilt; use a Band Aid. And thou shall not remove thy neighbour's landmark.'

'But it's the Sheraton,' said a voice.

'When thou goest to battle be not afraid, for the Lord is there to fight for you.'

And the Israelites said, 'Good, we'll stand and watch.'

'And any men in ye battle line, that hath betrothed a wife and not yet taken her, let him return to his house, lest he die in battle, and another man take her.'

And lo, the army of Israel disappeareth.

14. After extra time the Israelites beat the Canaanites and the Lord said, 'Thy beaten enemy will serve thee.'

'Twenty beers and three whiskies,' said the Israelites.

'Ye shall battle and destroy the Amorites, Perizzites, Hittites, Tottenham Hotspur, Arsenal, the Hivites and the Parasites.' The case was adjourned 'till after lunch. The Lord spake [spoke? speak?] 'When thou besiege a city, thou shalt not destroy the trees, for thou must eat of them.'

The Israelites gave a low moan. 'We have to eat trees, Lord?'

'Only trees that be not meat, thou shalt cut down.'

'What for?' said the Israelites.

'Bulwarks,' said the Lord.

'And bulwarks to you,' said the Israelites.

15. Of wars, the Lord spake from a deck chair. 'If seest among battle captives a beautiful woman thou desirest, take her home and shave her head.'

'Lord, that's kinky,' said the Israelites. 'More daddy.'

'Next,' said the Lord, 'pare her nails.'

'What about the black stockings and suspender belt?' cried the Israelites.

The Lord loseth heart, and was cast down. 'If', said the Lord, 'thou lose interest in her, let her go where she will; thou will not sell her for money, but charge by the hour, that or place her with the Alfred Marks Bureau. If a man have two wives, one beloved, and one hated.'

'Keep the ones with the big boobs,' said an Israelite voice.

16. 'Now', said the Lord from 300a Bargery Road, Catford, 'if a wife bear a son and he is stubborn and rebellious and will not obey – kill him.'

'Lord,' said the Israelites, 'is there no alternative?'

'Yes, there's always a recording contract. I am the Lord thy God, and a bit of a goer. If a man commit murder, hang him on a tree.'

'There are no trees in the desert, Lord,' said the Israelites.

'Then hang him on the wall.'

'Amen,' said the Israelites.

The Lord appeared in a pillar of cloud and couldn't see a thing: 'If thy brother's sheep go astray, bring them back to thy brother; the rate for finding sheep is three shekels an hour. The same applieth to thine brother's ass; thou must not be cruel and kick his ass. Thou shalt not plough with an ox and ass together because they go sideways . . . Thou shalt not wear a garment of divers sorts, as of woollen and leather together.'

'This will kill the trade,' said the Israelites.

17. The Lord appeared in a new ball of fire with better insulation and said, 'If a man taketh a wife, and go in unto her, and hate her . . .'

'Hard bloody luck,' said the Israelites.

The Lord said, 'If a man find a damsel that is a virgin and lay with her; he shall give her father a hundred silver shekels.'

'It's too much,' said a voice. 'We've seen her.'

'I am the Lord God who took you out of Egypt, etc., etc.'

'It's the commercial,' said the Israelites.

The Lord said, 'He that is wounded in the stones; or hath his privy member cut off, shall not enter the congregation.'

'It's his own fault,' said the Israelites; 'he kept a Rottweiler.'

18. 'If a man among you is not clean by reason of that which chanceth him in the middle of the night, then open all the windows and be rid of it. When evening come, let him goeth out the camp and wash his parts; when the sun is down, let him return to the camp with a room next to the WC.'

And they praised the Lord in his wisdom.

The Lord appeareth in a further pillar of cloud fitted with double glazing. 'Thou shalt have a place also without the camp, whither thou shall go abroad; it is called timeshare. And thou shalt have a paddle*, that when thou ease thyself abroad, thou shalt dig therewith, and shalt turn back and cover that which has come from thee. And let there be Andrex . . . Thou shalt not

* Shovel

71

bring the hire of a whore, or the price of a dog, into the house of the Lord.'

'Don't worry,' said the Israelites, 'we won't use your house.'

19. 'Tsu, tsu,' said the Lord, 'when thou shalt vow a vow unto the Lord, thou shalt not slack to pay it, and thou dost pay; it must be cash. When a man taketh a wife, and has found uncleanness in her, like the dishes, let him write her a bill of divorcement and send her out to post it, then change the locks on the doors. If she become another man's wife . . . '

'Sell him her clothes,' said the Israelites.

The Lord appeared in a Mark II fiery bush with asbestos shields: 'When a man taketh a new wife, he shall not go to war, neither shall he do any business but stay at home and cheer his wife.'

'Who'll look after the shop?' said the Israelites.

20. The Lord spoke. 'If a man stealeth from one of the children of Israel and maketh merchandise, he shall die unless he pay it all back with interest.'

'We'd rather die,' sayeth the children of Israel.

The Lord spoke, 'Take heed in the plague of leprosy, for if thine legs fall off surely thou has it. Now remember what the Lord thy God did unto Miriam after ye left Egypt.'

The children of Israel couldn't remember what God had done to Miriam, but many of the children of Israel doth gossip.

'If a man be poor, thou shalt not sleep with his pledge, but keep the ticket in the office. Remember the poor of the parish.'

'We are the poor of the parish,' said the children of Israel.

21. The Lord returned in a new pillar of cloud fitted with de-misters. 'If thou cuttest down the harvest put some aside for the stranger, the fatherless and the widow. If thou beatest thine olive trees, put some aside for the stranger, the fatherless and the widow. When thou gatherest grapes, put some aside for the stranger, the fatherless and the widow.'

The stranger, the fatherless and the widow then went on to open a thriving grocery shop.

The Lord spake, 'If a man like not to take his dead brother's wife, then shall his brother's wife go with him to the elders, loose his shoe from his foot and spit in his face, and for ever more his shall be called in Israel "the house of the man that hath his shoe loosed". [Big Deal.] When men strive together, the wife draweth near to her husband, putteth forth her hand and take him by the secrets.'

22. 'We come to weights and measures,' said the Lord, and a great hush fell over the children of Israel, many of whom kept shops. The Lord said, 'Thou shalt not have in thy bag divers weights, great and small.'

A shudder went though the children of Israel.

'Thou shalt have perfect measures and just weights.'

A great groan came from the children of Israel.

The Lord heard and said, 'Did I not bring you to the land of milk and honey?'

They said, 'Yes, Lord, but the milk goes off very quickly.'

The Lord was wrath, the Israelites were funnier than him. 'Remember what Amalek did unto thee when ye came forth from Egypt?'

No, the children of Israel couldn't remember, which was a pity because neither could God.

23. 'Now,' said the Lord, 'take the first fruits of the earth.'

'They're prunes, Lord,' said the Israelites.

'Take them unto the priest and he shall eat of them.'

And they took the prunes and the priest eateth them, and soon he got them badly.

'Remember,' said the Lord, 'I brought you out of the wilderness with outstretched arms and signs "This way to the milk and honey".' Then the Lord disappeared and was gone.

24. And the Israelites said, 'Look down on us, O Lord, and bless thy people that liveth in the land of milk and honey but what we want is oil.'

And Moses said, 'Hello, I'm back. This day thou art become the people of the Lord.'

'Do we have to sign anything?' said the children of Israel.

Moses said, 'Thou shall stand upon Mount Gerizim and curse the Canaanites.'

So the Israelites stood there and shouted, 'You Canaanites are a lot of bastards.'

Moses said, 'The law says cursed be the man who makes a graven image in a secret place like Golders Green post office.'

25. 'Cursed be he who setteth fire to his mother or

father. Cursed be he who removeth his neighbour's landmark, like Canary Wharf. Cursed be he who maketh the blind to wander out of his way, or under a bus. Cursed be he who lieth with his father's wife; because [wait for it] he uncovereth his father's skirt. Cursed be he who lieth with his mother-in-law.'

'Give him a medal,' said the Israelites.

Moses gave a smile – the only one in the whole Bible. 'Children,' he said, 'blessed shalt thou be in the city, blessed be thou in the field.'

'The city is better, there's more business,' said the Israelites.

'Blessed', said Moses, 'shalt thou be when thou comes in, blessed shall thou be when thou goest out.'

'What about when you're only halfway in and halfway out?' said the Israelites.

Moses turned a deaf ear and a rheumatic elbow. 'The Lord shall cause thine enemies that rise up against you to be smitten before your face.'

'We don't need any of that,' said the Israelites.

26. Moses went on: 'The Lord said thou shall lend unto many nations, but thou must not borrow.'

A groan of despair came from the children of Israel. 'The mortgage, what about the mortgage?' they wailed.

Moses said, 'The Lord shall make thee the head, and not the tail; thou shall be above only, and not be beneath.'

There was a pause and a voice said, 'He's pissed.'

Moses said, 'If you hearken not to the Lord, He will smite thee with a consumption, a fever, an inflammation, burning in the loins and mildew.'

'Who's going to argue?' said the Israelites.

27. Moses hadn't finished the threats. 'The Lord will cause thine enemy to punish thee. Thou will flee seven ways before them, mostly "B" roads. The Lord will smite thee with, and I have the list here: with the botch of Egypt, haemorrhoids, the scab and the itch. He will smite thee on the knees and in the legs with a sore botch that cannot be healed.'

'Thank God we're all on BUPA,' said the Israelites.

Moses said, 'The Lord will smite thee with madness.'

'Tell Him not to worry, we've got enough,' said the Israelites.

Moses went on: 'The Lord will smite thee with blindness; thou shall grope at midday.'

This frightened not the Israelites as they gropeth at all times.

The Lord said: 'Time will come when these things will come to you, the blessing and the curse.'

'Make up your mind, God,' said the Israelites. 'One day we're all sinners being cursed, the next day we're the chosen children of God; half of us are under a psychiatrist.'

28. The Lord heard them not as his pillar of cloud was soundproofed.

Moses came and spake unto all Israel. 'I am an hundred and twenty years old this day.'

'Happy birthday to you,' sang the crowd.

Moses said, 'I can no more go out or come in.'

'Then where are you?' said the Israelites.

Moses said, 'The Lord said I shall not go over the Jordan.'

Cries of Shame! and You need a holiday.

29. Moses said, 'The Lord shall go across the Jordan to the promised land and do all travel arrangements with Thomsons.'

And Moses said unto Joshua, 'Go thou to Jordan and prepare the land that the Israelites may possess it. Take a solicitor.'

And the Lord said unto Moses, 'Behold, the days approach when thou must die.'

'I know, Lord,' said Moses, 'that's why I sleep in a coffin.'

30. And the Lord appeared in the tabernacle in a pillar of cloud, and the pillar of cloud stood over the tabernacle causing condensation, rust, mildew and verdigris. And the Lord said unto Moses, 'Thou sleep with thy fathers.'

'Lord,' said Moses, 'there's only room for one in the coffin.'

31. In time the Lord would take His children unto the land of milk, honey and cholesterol. When Moses had finished the law book, he offered it to Michael Joseph, who published it under the pen name of Jeffrey Archer. And he placed publishers' copies on the ark of the covenant at a knockdown price of £7.50. And he spoke to the Levites who carry the ark. 'I know thy rebellion and stiff neck; believe me, it's better than piles.' Here he inserteth a suppository. 'Call all the elders of the tribe that I may speak words in their ears or any other orifice that works.'

32. 'Remember the days of old, consider the years of

old generations, ask thy father and he will show you rheumatism. Jacob is the Lord's inheritance. He found him in a desert, a real yobbo, in the waste of a howling dead land, East Ham, he crieth out '' 'ere we go, 'ere we go, 'ere we go'', but the Lord quietened him with six packs of Fosters, and He instructeth him in the ways of the Lord.'

Moses paused to take a Novmison and said, 'As an eagle stirreth up her nest over her young, spreadeth her wings, taketh her young and bear them on her wings.' [Wrong. There is no record of an eagle carrying her chicks on her wings.]

Moses groaned, 'Don't quote me,' he said, 'I'm under contract to Penguin.' He continued in the death-is-apparent position. 'The Lord took Jacob and made him ride the highest places on earth, where he nearly died through lack of oxygen, he made him suck honey [wait for it] out of the rock, and oil out of the flinty rod.'

What he needed was a rig.

33. The Lord said, 'Fire is kindled in mine anger and set on fire, the foundations of the mountains. They shall be burnt with hunger, devoured with burning heat, all will be destruction. I will send the teeth of beasts upon them, the sword without, the terror within, all will die the young man, the virgin, the man with grey hairs.'

'Same time tomorrow, Lord?' sayeth Moses.

The children of Israel were wrath. This Lord, one day He's okay, next day He's going to set fire to the world, was He on something?

The Lord started early the next day at 6.30. 'To me belongeth vengeance.'

'He's off again,' said the Israelites.

'Silence,' said the Lord.

34. 'Thine religion is thy rock – that rock shall be all the hours of the day.'

'Lord,' said the baffled Israelites, 'does that mean rock around the clock?'

The Lord in his pillar of cloud smote His chest as He knew not what the children of Israel meant, relations were strained, they were put in a muslin bag and squeezed.

The Lord said, 'I lift up my hand to heaven and say I live forevermore.'

Genealogists say there is no evidence of a man holding up his hand to heaven has ever lived for ever, the oldest was ninety-three and came from Slough. Moses said, 'Beware of all that is false.'

'Does that go for teeth?' said the Israelites.

Moses said, 'The Lord came from Sinai and He came with ten thousand saints, though a poll only showed three hundred; the rest were workers for Datsun on a day out.'

35. From the Lord's right hand went a fiery law.

The Israelites were glad they had fitted smoke detectors. And of Levi, the Lord said, 'Let thy Thummim and Urim be. I'll say that again, Thummim and Urim be thy holy one. Thou shalt put incense before thee and put the whole burnt sacrifice on thine altar. Let Reuben live and not die.'

'Why me?' said Reuben. [Who he?]

The Lord worked in mysterious ways and these were some of them.

Moses said, 'To the Lord belongeth vengeance [again?], thy foot will slide in due time – because there's a lot of it about.'

36. A Levi sayeth unto his father, 'I have not seen him.'

'Seen who?' sayeth his father.

'I don't know,' said Levi, 'all I know, whoever it is I have not seen him.' Neither did he acknowledge his brethren, nor knew his own children. The doctors diagnosed amnesia. 'Bless the Lord and his substance, which I think is Polyfilla, smite the loins of them against thee, which usually cripples 'em, praise the Lord. His glory is like the firsting of his bullocks. He shall push the people together to the ends of the earth.'

'They'll fall off,' said the Israelites.

Moses said, 'And of Benjamin, the Lord shall cover him all day, and he shall dwell between his shoulders.'

So Benjamin got between his shoulders and lived.

37. 'For the righteousness, they shall suck an abundance of the sea, and treasures hid in the sand, like lug worms.' Of Gad he said: 'He dwelleth like a lion, and teareth the arm with the crown of his head.'

'He must be deformed,' said the Israelites.

And of Dan, he said, 'He's a lion's whelp: he shall leap from Mount Bashan.'

'The fall will kill him,' said the children of Israel.

Moses still went on: 'Of Naphtali: possess thou the west and the south, thus avoiding the awful Northern Line.'

38. And of Asher: 'Let him be acceptable to his brethren, let him dip his foot in oil, using 3 in One.'

'That's no good,' cried the children of Israel, 'we need a rig!'

Moses said, 'Children of Israel, thy shoes will be iron and brass.'

The children of Israel beat their chests and shouted, 'It's time you retired.'

Moses didn't retire, instead he said, 'Israel shall dwell in a land of corn and wine.'

'What happened to the milk and honey?' said the Israelites.

'It's crop rotation,' said Moses.

39. And Moses went up the mountain and the Lord showed him all the land of Gilead, unto Dan, all Naphtali, all Catford and Lewisham. 'This is the land which I swore unto Abraham.'

'It's enough to make anyone swear,' said Moses; then he died.

He was a hundred and twenty when he died. His eye was not dim, nor his natural force abated, but the drink finally got him. He was buried in the land of Moab, leaving many unpaid bills and maintenance orders.

❈ CHAPTER VIII ❈

THE NEW WONDER BOY WAS JOSHUA, he would plague the Israelites like Moses had, and prepareth to cross the Jordan. Joshua sent two men out of Shittim to spy out the land and house prices. And the two men lodged in the house of a harlot named Rahab; after a week they were still there, all the spying they did was through key holes. The king of Jericho came unto Rahab.

'Same again?' she said.

The king was wrath as he hadn't got time. 'Bring forth the spies that have come unto ye.'

But Rahab couldn't lose such good customers and lieth; 'They have fled.' Rahab had hidden them in the rafters among the pigeons; they were covered in it. She let them down on a rope from the window, but meeteth the king of Jericho coming the other way, and they runneth like fuck. And they cometh back to Joshua and tell him the land over there is good and they're ready for a takeover. They said they'd already taken over Rahab.

2. Joshua rose early in the morning and removed from Shittim and came to Jordan. The children of Israel lodged there, passed over or out. The officers went

through the host as it was an all-ticket match. Joshua said, 'Tomorrow the Lord will do wonders among you.'

'Can He do something about the rates?' said the children of Israel.

Joshua said, 'God without fail will drive out the Canaanites, the Hittites, the Catholics, the CofE and the Methodists. Now, take you twelve men out of the tribes of Israel.'

'Who are we playing?' said the children of Israel.

Joshua said to the priests, 'Take up the ark and pass over before the people.'

So they took up the ark and passed over before the people. It was simple, all they had to do was to take up the ark and pass over before the people.

3. Joshua said to the priests that took the ark and passed over before the people, 'When ye come to the River Jordan, ye shall stand still in it.'

'But it's bloody cold,' said the priests, who had taken up the ark and passed over the people.

The Lord said: 'When the ark reaches the Jordan the waters shall be cut off.'

'You hear that,' said Mrs Cohen, 'they're going to cut the water off.'

4. Like the Red Sea the Lord divided the water and the children of Israel, after passport control, passed through. At that time the Lord said unto Joshua, 'Make the knives sharp and circumcise again the children of Israel the second.'

From those who had been done once came a cry, 'Not again.'

So Joshua circumcised the children of Israel at the hill of the foreskins, now the holiday town of Eilat.

5. Now Jericho City would not allow the children of Israel free passage. The Lord said unto Joshua, 'I give into thine hand Jericho.'

'Ta,' said Joshua.

The Lord then spoke from the changing rooms at Lord's Pavilion, 'Take thou thy priests with rams' horn trumpets and the children of Israel, circle the city of Jericho seven times, then blow thy trumpets and let the children of Israel give a great shout and Jericho will crumble.'

So Joshua did so, on the seventh lap at midnight they blew the trumpets and shoutest, and, lo, the walls came down showing most of the citizens caught in flagrante delicto, except Rahab who was resting. And they burnt the city with fire [what else], all except Rahab's house.

6. Only the silver and gold, and the vessels of brass and iron, were put into the 'treasury of the house of the Lord' [said Joshua], which appeared to be on a sheet in his bathroom cupboard.

The Lord spoke, 'Cursed be he that rebuildeth Jericho.'

A great groan went up from the Association of Israelite Builders. But the children of Israel committed a trespass in the accursed thing [dear reader, over to you].

7. Now Joshua sent men to go to Ai, and they went up and saw the lights were still on in Rahab's house. They said, 'Send two or three thousand soldiers and smite Ai.'

CHAPTER VIII

So Joshua sent up three thousand soldiers and the people of Ai smote them [beat the shit out of them]. Joshua rent his clothes before the Lord and fell to the earth upon his face, and put dust on his head: a one hundred per cent grovel.

The Lord said, 'Get up. Why liest thou upon thy face?'

'It seemed the right thing to do at the time,' said Joshua.

8. And when the children of Israel knew the Ai had beaten their army, the children of Israel rent their clothes; they also rented their furniture. 'O Lord,' said Joshua, 'what shall I say when the Israelites turn their back on their enemy?'

'About turn,' said the Lord.

Joshua said, 'The Canaanites have cut off our name from the earth.'

And the Lord said, 'With aerosol spray you can redo it.' The Lord then spoke from a wool shed in Yatatonga. 'There is an accursed thing in thy midst, thou art cursed until you find this accursed thing.'

And they searched all night and, lo, they findeth the accursed thing; it was a pound of bacon. Joshua cursed Mrs Cohen, and with the priests they stoned the pound of bacon to death. Mrs Cohen wept bitterly. 'It was a special offer,' she moaned.

9. It came to pass, a boy Achan confessed that he had stolen from the prisoners a good Babylonish jacket, two hundred shekels of silver and a wedge of gold. Joshua was wrath. He took the stolen goods, laid them out on the back of his chariot and a good boot sale was

had by all with Joshua five hundred pounds up on the day. Then he took Achan and gave him a jolly good stoning.

10. Now the kings hereabout saw what Joshua did to the Ai. Verily, he beateth the shit out of them, some of the Insurance Companies refuseth to pay some of the claims, so spies were sent to check on the children of Israel's army. Joshua saw them and said, 'Who are ye?'

They said, 'Ahem, we are a band of strolling singers.'

Joshua, he loveth music and bid the strolling singers to sing, so they singeth and Joshua had them stoned to death, but they escapeth unto the house of Rahab, which was a no-go area. It was known these men were spies from the king of Ai so Joshua led his army against the Ai and burnt it and made it an heap for ever, even a desolation unto this day and it is called Camden Town. And the king of Ai hanged on a tree 'till eventide; then the body was taken down, thrown at the city gates, and raised thereon a great heap of stones, known to this day as East Finchley.

11. And from the prisoners there were hewers of wood, drawers of water, fixers of plumbing, unblockers of WCs, launderers and ironers. But prisoners were wrath. 'Among us there are princes and kings.'

'Hard bloody luck,' said Joshua.

12. And it came to pass, the men of Gibeon called to Joshua, 'Help, we are being attacked by the Amorites.' Joshua rose up, not too nigh, just enough to walk; he arriveth at Gibeon, but God had already smote the Amonites hip and thigh [that's where most of the inju-

ries were] but, lo, the Lord sayeth, 'Sun, stand still,'
and it stood still. So there was extra time for Joshua to
destroy the Amorites and go late shopping. Every now
and then the Lord smote one or two with a hail of
rocks. And there was no day like that before it or after
it [eh?].

13. Now it came to pass, Joshua and the children of
Israel stopped slaying the enemy only because there
were no more left, but five kings had been captured,
and Joshua made them lie prostrate and Joshua walketh
on their necks, a real crowd pleaser. For an encore he
slew them. When the applause died down, he cast them
into a cave and blocked it with rocks. And the Lord
blessed him and his people.

14. And afterwards Joshua read the words of the law
the blessings and the cursing [bugger, damn, blast].
And that day Joshua took Makkedah, smote it with the
edge of the sword; he utterly destroyed them. Next, it
was Libnah's turn, which was Israel 6 Libnah 1 [own
goal]. Then Joshua destroyed Lachish, Israel 7 Lachish
1. He and the Israelites went on to destroy Eglon,
Hebron, Debir; and everywhere the Israelites were victorious because, though it seemed a bit unfair, the Lord
God fought for them and He had archangels on the
substitute bench. So Joshua and the Israelites went on
devastating the country; with God on their side they
couldn't lose.

15. God egged him on: 'Be not afraid because of
them; I will deliver them up all slain, and burn their
houses and chariots with fire; they will be oven-ready.'

The Israelites went on to exterminate Jazer, Gilead, Ammon, Aroer, Heshbon, Betonim.

Joshua said, 'Lord, we're getting tired.'

The Lord said, 'Verily, yes, exterminate the Rekenites and we'll call it a day.' So the smiting and smoting was on again.

16. Joshua called the tribes of Israel together to discuss Moses' will and inheritance. The Levis got the mantelpiece clock, the Manasseh got the fish knives and forks, the Reubens got the ass, the Jacobs got the wardrobe. The Cohens got the three flying ducks and the barometer (slightly broken). And the Lord blessed them and their inheritances. He was interrupted by a cry of 'What about the fur coats?' The meeting was closed and Joshua went off a-smiting and a-smoting. The Lord God went before him on a pillar of cloud now fitted with a periscope.

17. Now Joshua was old and stricken in years; it was all shrivelled up. The Lord said, 'Thou are old and stricken in years and it's all shrivelled up.'

'I'm all right with a zimmer,' said Joshua, and the Lord blessed his zimmer.

The Lord said, 'There is still land not distributed among the tribes; the surveyor is working on it now. The going price per acre with outline planning permission is a thousand shekels. Land is vacant from Aphek to the borders of the Amorites and Bradford and the Pakistanis who dwell in corner shops.'

18. Unto the tribe of Levi Moses' will left them nothing: the Lord God was their inheritance. And Mr

Levi was heard to moan, 'You can't draw cheques on someone on a pillar of cloud.'

Joshua said, 'Forty years old was I when Moses PLC sent me to espy out the land; and I told him the land was going for a song, then and there he sang it. And Moses swore on that day – "bugger" he said.' Joshua went on, 'Behold, the Lord and steroids have kept me alive. I am as strong this day as I was in Moses' day, thanks to a pacemaker.'

19. The last of Moses' will was that the children of Judah would own land from Ged even unto the border of Edom, who was renting the top bedroom and did it out the window. He was known as the Dir-tee-Barger.

20. At that time Othniel, brother of Caleb, sons of Kenaz, gave his daughter Achsah, to wife. She came afar and she lighted off her ass; there was smoke everywhere. Caleb said, 'What wouldst thou?'

She said, 'You can put this ass out.'

So he sprayed the ass. 'Now what?' he sayeth.

She sayeth, 'Give me springs of water.'

He gave her the upper springs, and the nether springs; she falleth in.

21. And now all Moses' will had been read and final land division went to Shiorn; his land was from Aroer to a bank on the Jordan – a bank where he was heavily overdrawn. And Joshua swore that surely wherever thy feet have trodden shall be thy land. As he spoke all the children of Israel were walking the land in size fourteen boots. Joshua's fee for this advice was twenty per cent of the selling price.

22. It came to pass, a lot of children of Joseph fell from Jordan by Jericho, unto the water of Jericho. Lo, they goeth in dry and cometh out soaked. And the priests were wrath and sayeth, 'This is Sunday, a holy day of obligation: no swimming allowed.'

The children cried, 'You want us to drown.'

And the priest said, 'Yes, drowning is allowed of a Sunday.'

The Lord appeared in a pillar of cloud. It came to pass, the Lord gave peace to the Israelites, having exterminated every living tribe. Joshua waxed old and stricken with age, awaiting a hip operation, teeth and a wig. He called all the elders together. 'I am old and stricken with age.'

'Have you tried cod-liver oil?' said the elders.

'The Lord has fought for us, keep in with Him; He likes burnt offerings; He loves chicken livers. If you need help, call Him and He will slayeth whoever you want.'

'How about bank managers?' said the elders.

Joshua said, 'The Lord in past times took Abraham, led him throughout the land of Canaan, and multiplied his seed with grow bags.'

23. Then Jacob and the children of Israel went down to Egypt 3 Israel Nil. 'Hear now, it shall come to pass all good things are from the Lord, but shall the Lord bring upon you evil things until He hath destroyed you from this good land.'

'He must be meshuga,' said the elders.

Joshua said, 'If ye forsake the Lord and serve strange gods, don't use the good silver.'

CHAPTER VIII

24. And it came to pass that Joshua died; people who knew said it was the booze. They buried him next to the border, who had died owing three weeks' rent. On the Monday they held the sale; the biggest item was Joshua's copy of the Ten Commandments, which were auctioned off singly.

CHAPTER IX

NOW A NEW LEADER CAME TO THE CHILDREN OF ISRAEL, Judah, and he went and smote the Canaanites — but their king Adonibezek fled, but they caught him, cut off his thumbs and great toes. And Adonibezek said, 'Threescore and ten kings, having their thumbs and their great toes cut off, gathered their meat under my table.'

'Oh, kinky eh?' said Judah.

2. Now the children of Kenite went out of the city and they went and settled among the peace-loving people of Arad. Judah came with his brother, and slew them and utterly destroyed it.

And the Lord said, 'This is Judah with whom I am well pleased.'

3A. There wast a time when the children of Israel were slaves for the king of Moab, but the children of Israel cried out to the Lord, 'HELLLULPP!'

The Lord heard and spoke to them, 'I will rise up a champion for you.'

3B. And He rose up Ehud. Ehud made a Swiss Army knife. When he'd finished he made his way into the king's chamber and said to the king, 'I have a present for you,' and stuck the dagger in the king's belly.

'You call this a present? It's very dangerous,' said the king and died.

Ehud then ran up a mountain, blew a ram's horn and shouted to the children of Israel, 'You are free.' And the Lord blessed Ehud, his Swiss Army knife, his ram's horn, and his psychiatrist.

3C. But the Israelites forsook the Lord, and the anger of the Lord was hot against Israel, and He delivered the Israelites into the hands of spoilers that spoiled them, and the Lord sold them into the hands of the enemy, but as they were so spoilt He didn't get many offers and the Israelites went a-whoring all in the month of May. And the Lord paced the floor of His pillar of cloud and He swore against them.

4. The children of Israel now dwelt among Canaanites, Hittites and Amorites, but they sent their children to a private school. The Israelites again did evil in the sight of the Lord.

'If only they'd pull the blinds,' He said.

5. Deborah was the prophetess at the time the Israelites came up to her for judgement. Usually she gave six months, the others got off with a fine. Deborah called Barak, the Israelite general, who said, 'I am about to exterminate Sisera and his army.'

'Good luck,' she said.

'No,' said Barak, 'if thou wilt go with me in my chariot, I will go; if you wilt not go with me in my chariot, I will not go.'

'That seems clear; boring but clear. Yes, I will come but my going rate is ten shekels a mile.'

'It's a bit much,' said Barak.

'I know,' said Deborah; 'that's why I charge it.'

Alas, Sisera and his army were thrashed. Sisera fled on his feet and Jael, the wife of Heber, gave Sisera succour and rested him in her tent. She offered him salt beef sandwiches and covered him with a velvet mantle. He said to her, 'If any man ask of me, say I am not here,' and he slept. Jael took a nail off the tent pole and took a hammer. She went softly to him and smote the nail unto his temples. So he died and Jael put her B&B signs outside her tent again.

6. Deborah, who had walked back from the battle, checked the meter on the late Sisera's chariot; it showed one thousand nine hundred shekels. 'You'll never see that now,' said Jael. Jael took Barak and said, 'Come, I will show you the man thou seek,' and he came in the tent and there lay Sisera dead with nails in his temple.

Barak said to her, 'Tell me, what were you trying to make?'

7. Under a date palm, which was a low rental property, Deborah sang praises. Her voice made you think her fanny was on fire. 'Hear, O ye kings; give ear.'

'Give over,' said the Israelites.

'Lord,' said Deborah, 'when thou marchedst out, the earth trembled, the heavens dropped, the clouds also dropped water, and there was a prediction of an early frost with snow on high ground.'

And the Lord appeared in a new enlarged pillar of cloud as He had friends in.

Deborah sang the praise of Jael, how she killed

Sisera. 'At her feet', she sang, 'he bowed [all with a nail in his nut], he fell, he lay down [tra la la, the blood running down his face]: where he bowed, there he fell down dead [tra la la la la].' This song went straight into the charts; there was nowhere else for it to go.

8A. And the Bible says, Awake, awake Deborah from under your palm tree awake, awake, utter a song, arise. Deborah sang of the late-night revellers. 'Ye that ride white asses, get thine asses out of here.' And it came to pass that kings came and fought. They took no gain of money, but there was a silver collection in the interval. To the Israelites the Lord spoke from a burning bush with air-conditioning. 'I am thy Lord God, but ye have not obeyed my voice.'

'Well, you haven't given us any orders,' said the Israelites.

8B. And there was Gideon, who threshed wheat at night by the wine vat, in case customs officers came looking for an illicit still.

And the angel of the Lord said unto him, 'The Lord is with thee, thou mighty man of valour.'

'Gee, thanks,' said Gideon. 'Can you fill in the details?'

9. The angel crossed his legs [poor circulation]. 'Thou Gideon will save Israel.'

'Hasn't it been saved enough?' said Gideon.

'Thou shall smite the Midianites as one man,' said the angel.

'I *am* only one man,' said Gideon.

The angel of the Lord uncrossed his legs.

Gideon said, 'If I'm to smite, smeet and smote the Midianites, then shew me a sign from the Lord that thou talkest with me.'

And the angel said, 'Thou will have a sign 6 x 4 saying "This way to the battle".'

Then Gideon made ready a kid, half a pound unleavened cakes of ephah flour; 4 oz the flesh, and two veg. He put them in a basket and broth in a pot. 'I've brought lunch for the Lord,' said Gideon. The angel of the Lord said, 'Place all the food on that rock.'

Gideon did so.

The angel touched the meal with a staff. Lo, great flames burst from the rock and burnt the meal to ashes. The angel of the Lord departed out of sight.

10. Gideon swore and said, 'I'll get him for this.'

The Lord said, 'Peace on you.'

Gideon said, 'Peace on you too.'

Then Gideon said, 'Why did thou burn the lunch?'

And the Lord said, 'There was a breakdown in communications and there's no such thing as a free lunch; fear not, thou shalt not die.'

'Oh, ta,' said Gideon.

Israel: It is reported that today three hundred Israelite troops under Gideon drove the Midianites from the village. Most of them were slewn and slain, casualties among Israelite forces were light. God has blessed Gideon personally.

11. Gideon had the wind and let go a blast on his trumpet and was much relieved, but it cleared the room. And Gideon came to the Jordan, he and his three

hundred men passed over. Many were faint with hunger, and he asked the people of Succoth for bread.

'Dost thou want white or wholemeal?' they asked.

'Wholemeal,' said Gideon; 'it's higher in fibre.'

But the princes of Succoth sayeth, 'Ye have attacked our allies, the Midianites. Why should we give you bread?'

Gideon was wrath. 'When I have slain the Midianites, I will tear your flesh with thorns of the wilderness.'

'Oh, you spiteful little swine,' said the princes.

Gideon then went unto the men of Penuel and they told him to piss off.

Gideon said, 'When this war is over, I'll break down this tower.' And the Penuel said, 'Thou canst, it is Listed Grade One.'

12. And Gideon was sore afraid. He went on and slew a few more Midianites, and they surrendered and said, 'Sorry.'

Then Gideon said, 'Will every woman throw down her earrings.' And the weight of the golden earrings came to one thousand seven hundred shekels, which Gideon deposited with the Bradford and Bingley. Thus were the Midianites subdued, and lifted up their heads no more and kept walking into lampposts. Gideon had threescore and ten sons and a worn willy for he had many wives. Gideon died at a great age and had to be lifted off. As soon as Gideon was dead, the children of Israel went worshipping Baalberith and went a-whoring, a good time was had by all.

13. The next Biblical butcher was Abimelech, the son

of Jerubbaal. He said, 'Who shall lead you, my forty brothers or me?'

And they said, 'You.'

He said, 'I'll need expenses.' So they drew forty shekels from the Halifax. With this he hired some men, they all went into his father's house and slew his brethren, leaving a note on the mantelpiece saying there'd be forty fewer for dinner.

14. For this work, they made Abimelech king; in those distant Biblical days promotion came very quickly. One didn't become a prince first and wait for mother to die. And the elders spoke to a tree asking if Abimelech was a wise choice. 'If ye have dealt truly with Jerubbaal, then let him be king, if not, let fire come out from Abimelech.' As it spoke, Abimelech's trousers caught fire and through the screams came the smell of burning hairs. And Jotham [whoever he was] fled with his trousers on fire and stayed long in the River Jordan, cooling his scorched parts. Apart from a funny walk, Abimelech reigned three years without being tumbled. Then God [yes, He's back on the scene folks] sent an evil spirit between Abimelech and the men of Shechem. It was an English plumber who whispered into Abimelech's ear: ''Ere, you didn't 'arf do up your bruvvers proper.'

15. Abimelech was afeared and clenched the cheeks of his bum together. There rose up among the people a young solicitor called Gaal and he fortified a city. But Abimelech laid siege to the city and Gaal shouted from the ramparts, 'You'll be charged with breaking and entering *and* GBH.'

A certain woman cast a millstone on Abimelech and it broke his head. 'You'll pay for this,' he shouted at the woman.

'No, no,' she cried, 'I did it for free.'

Abimelech said, 'I am dying, tell my wife the rent money is in the tea caddy.' So died a tyrant; the woman went on to become Mrs Thatcher.

16. And the children of Israel, egged on by the English plumber, did evil again, and the Lord's anger was hot against Israel [but cool round the back] and He sold them into the hands of the Philistines. The sale price was not revealed, and the Israelites were woe, and the Lord said, 'Did I not deliver you from the Egyptians?'

'Yes, yes, we know all that, what about this?'

17. Now Jephthah was a mighty man, chest expanded forty-five inches. He was the son of a harlot, his foster mother had two sons. They thrust Jephthah out of the home via the cat flap because: 'Thou art the son of a "strange woman".' He fled to the land of Tob and there gathered 'vain men', who went out with him and they sayeth, 'Verily, he must be gay.'

18. 'Ammon declares war on Israel,' said the *Jewish Chronicle*. Lo, the elders of Israel ran like the clappers to Jephthah, chest expanded forty-five inches and asked him to lead the Israelites. 'Do you know my mother was strange?'

'That's what they're saying about you,' said the elders.

'Yea, I will lead the Israelites, but it's five shekels an hour and I want a meter on my chariots.'

A three-year contract was signed with a get-out clause. And yet again Jephthah smote the Ammonites; this was the ninetieth time they'd been smoted. Jephthah rode his chariot over them at three shekels a mile.

19. Having beaten the shit out of the Ammonites he returned home. Behold, his daughter came out to greet him with timbrels and with dances. 'It's the latest craze, Dad,' she said.

'Get dressed at once,' he said. 'Go; go to the mountains and bewail your virginity for two months.' So she went but came back bewailing the loss of her virginity.

20. In time Jephthah becameth old in his time and he snuffeth it. And the children of Israel wailed as there were still debts outstanding. He left no money for his funeral so he was burned in a paper bag. Straightaway, oh woe, the children of Israel did evil in the sight of the Lord. He couldn't help seeing them on His pillar of cloud, which now had wraparound windows. 'You dirty little devils,' He shouteth out to them. And the Lord was wrath as they make certain signs at Him.

21. There was a man named Manoah; his wife was barren even though he tried testosterone. An angel of the Lord appeared unto the woman and said, 'Thou shall bear a son; I pray thee, drink not wine nor strong drink.'

The woman ran and fetched her husband and they saw the angel and Manoah said, 'You say my wife will bear a child – is this private or National Health?'

'She must not drink wine or strong drink,' said the angel.

'Does that go for me too?' said Manoah.

The angel said, 'No.'

'Would you stay for a burnt offering?' said Manoah.

'Nay, you must make it to the Lord. A light supper would do.'

22. So Manoah took a leg of lamb, half a pound of potatoes, 2 oz chopped carrots, and he put them on the fire on a rock to simmer for half an hour. It came to pass, a flame shot up from the rock towards heaven, taking the angel and the dinner with it. And Manoah and his wife both fell on their faces on the ground. Manoah said, 'We have seen God, surely we must die.'

'No, no,' said his wife. 'No, you don't die from God, you die from bronchitis.' In time the woman bore a son, and the father got bronchitis. They called the child Samson for that was his name. And Samson grew until he was inside leg thirty-nine. And Samson went down to Timnath and saw a woman inside leg thirty-eight. And he told his father that he had seen this Philistine woman and would wed her. His father, in between coughing, was wrath. 'Why pick ye a woman from the uncircumcised Philistines; when she sees yours she will surely faint.'

23. So Samson, his mother and father went down to Timnath and, behold, a young lion sprang on them. And Samson rent the lion and said, 'Look, folks, it's rent-a-lion.' Samson went down and talked with the woman and she pleased him much; it only took twenty minutes. He turned to see the carcase of the lion; in it was a swarm of bees and honey – it was the start of Tate & Lyle.

24. And Samson made a feast for the woman and she brought thirty companions. Samson said, 'I'll spin ye a riddle: if you get it right, I'll give you thirty changes of underwear, if you can't, I get thirty changes of underwear. This be the riddle: out of the calf came forth meat, out of the strong came forth sweetness. Get it?' They did not get it, so he killed thirty of them. Meanwhile, his wife had gone off with another. So Samson caught three hundred foxes, tied firebrands to their tails and, when the fire reached their bums, they ran off, setting fire to the cornfields. Then three thousand men of Judah came, bound him, and handed him over to the Philistines, and he was shamed as they were not circumcised. He broke his bonds and, with the jawbone of an ass, he killed another three thousand. He was arrested on two counts of GBH, cruelty to animals and in possession of an unlicensed jawbone of an ass.

25. And the Philistines imprisoned him and put in with him Delilah, who asked him where his strength lay. He told her until recently Lloyds of London – but that his real strength lay in his hair. She waiteth until he sleepeth, then she shaveth it off. Samson awoke and cried out, 'I'm bald, Lord! I'm bald.' The Philistines blinded him, they loved way-out jokes. But Samson took hold of the pillars of the building and down they came, causing several casualties; after hospital treatment they were allowed to go home. Samson ended his days a nightwatchman at Tate & Lyle – no one ever laughed at his riddle.

26. And there was a man who liveth on top of

Mount Ephraim because he said it made him look taller. His name was Micah. He sayeth, 'The eleven hundred shekels of silver that were stolen from thee: I believe it was mother.'

She said, 'Blessed be thou of the Lord, thou thieving little bastard.' She took back two hundred shekels, which she put into the high interest account at the Midland. For his share, Micah had graven images; he made an ephod from bonded resin and a teraphim from green plastic, both from DIY kits.

27. In those days there were no kings in Israel, and only one constable, so every man did what was right in his own eyes. Some did it by day, others by night with the blinds down. A certain Levite took to himself a concubine. She played the whore, she also played the banjo and harmonium, she spurned his advances, she did about ten spurns a day, then he stopped making advances and started to retreat. It all ended coitus interruptus, she left for her father's home taking her ass with her, not until she reached his house did she get off her ass. She was away four months, during this time the Levite maketh a rug, then he arose in the general direction of up and went after her. She took him to her father who rejoiced at having a new B&B customer and they sat down, ate and drank excellent. It was late when the Levite went to bed and later still when the landlord slipped the bill under his bedroom door.

28. And when the Levite rose up to depart, his father-in-law said, 'No, stay on, you'll be better off and so will I.' So he stayeth and the money runneth out and his father-in-law said, 'Isn't it time you left?'

So he taketh his concubine and they left for Mount Ephraim. Behold, there came an old man from a field where he'd been doing it. He said, 'Whither goest thou, and when comest thou?'

And the Levite sayeth, 'We know not whether we be coming or going.'

The old man rubbeth his eyes, 'I keep seeing spots before the eyes.'

They sayeth, 'Hast thou seen a doctor?'

He sayeth, 'No, only spots before the eyes.' Despite this terrible joke, the old man took them to his home. They washed their feet and the water turneth to porridge.

29. Then the sons of Belial came to the door asking for the Levite, but the old man telleth him not; instead he brought the concubine, and they abused her all night until the morning, when by now the sons of Belial had all caught it. And at the dawning of the day the Levite said, 'What have they done to her?'

'Everything,' said the old man.

The Levite took his dead concubine home, then he took a knife and cut her into twelve pieces and posted them, labelled P A L, to different dogs' homes. The Levite told the children of Israel what the sons of Belial had done to his concubine; he didn't tell them what *he'd* done to her.

30. The children of Israel arose, then beat the shit out of the sons of Belial. And the Lord blessed the children of Israel from His recently refurbished pillar of cloud.

❦ CHAPTER X ❦

THERE WAS NAOMI AND HER TWO WIDOWED DAUGHTERS-IN-LAW, Orpah and Ruth. There was famine in the land save food parcels from Oxfam. The *Jewish Chronicle* said that the Lord was in Moab distributing bread. Naomi was short of bread, smoked salmon, blintzes and soured cream. So she departeth, saying to Ruth, 'Thou need not come with me.'

But Ruth sayeth, 'Whither thou goest, I will go; thy people shall be my people.'

'That's very nice of you,' sayeth Naomi.

'I haven't finished yet,' said Ruth. 'When thou diest, I will die.'

'No, no, that's silly,' said Naomi. 'You die when it's your turn, eh?'

2. And they arriveth in Bethlehem. Ruth findeth work as a reaper of corn, and the owner of the field was Boaz. He said unto his reapers, 'The Lord be with you at one shekel a day.'

And they sayeth, 'It's bloody slavery.'

Boaz asked, 'Who is yon woman with the big ones?'

And he sayeth to her, 'Thou workest well, and I have charged my young men not to touch thee.'

'Did you have to?' said Ruth.

'If you wish, thou canst dwell in my home with my daughters, who are all straight.'

3. In gratitude, Ruth threw herself on her face on the ground.

'You won't see much there,' said Boaz.

She said, 'Why have I found grace in thine eyes?'

'There must be some mistake,' said Boaz; 'I haven't got anything called grace in mine eyes. Now, at meal-times come you hither, to eat, and to dip thy morsel in the vinegar.'

So Ruth had to be satisfied with morsels and dipped vinegar. Ruth returneth to the shekel-a-day reaping and she reapeth an ephah of barley and gave the ephah to Naomi. She maketh an ephah cake and eateth it; Ruth got bugger-all.

4. 'Where thou goest, I goest,' said Ruth.

'That's awkward,' said Naomi, 'I'm going to the loo.'

Ruth said, 'I must return to Mr Boaz, who looketh after me.'

Naomi said, 'Show thou respect for Boaz, wash thyself and anoint thee and put a raiment upon thee, and get thee down to the floor. And when Mr Boaz lieth down, mark thou the place he shall lie, then go in, and uncover his feet, and lay thee down; and he will tell thee what to do.'

'You must be bloody mad,' said Ruth.

And Naomi weepeth.

Cometh a happy ending. Ruth went and did as Naomi said, and when she uncovered Mr Boaz's feet, it turned him on. 'Do it again,' he said, and married her. After a night of foot uncovering, he begat her and she bore a son. He was called Obed, and his genealogical tree was: Pharez begat Hezron, who begat Ram, and Ram begat Amminadab, who begat Nahshon, who begat Salmon, who begat Boaz, who begat Obed.

AND THERE CAME A MAN, ELKANAH; to his wives and children, he gave portions. To his wife Hannah who had no children he gave a worthy portion, about one pound three ounces. What the portions were the Bible doesn't say. But Hannah was low because the Lord God shut up her womb. And Hannah spoke in her heart; only her lips moved, and Eli [who he?] said unto her, 'How long wilt thou be drunken?'

And Hannah said, 'I have drunk neither wine nor strong drink like Vodka or Jack Daniels to God. I have poured out my soul, that and a cup of Twinings' Earl Grey.' That night, Elkanah, Hannah's husband, knew* his wife, and she beareth a son, Samuel – who would one day refuse to pick up his musket. And Hannah rejoiceth; she prayed. 'Lord, mine horn is exalted; I shall play it at parties; neither is there any rock like our Lord, rock on then.'

2. Hannah spoke to Eli; it was forty-four pence a minute. 'The Lord killeth, and maketh alive: He bringeth down to the grave and bringeth them up.'

* Had it away with

'Why does he want to bring them up again, aren't they dead enough?'

Hannah went on. 'He raiseth up the poor from the dust, and lifteth the beggar from the dunghill, and set them among the princes.'

'God,' said Eli, 'what about the smell, Andrew, for one, wouldn't like?'

Hannah sayeth, 'He will keep the feet of his saints.'

'They won't get far,' said Eli.

Hannah sayeth, 'The adversaries of the Lord shall be broken to pieces.'

'There's Super Glue,' said Eli.

3. A priest's custom, when any man offered dinner, the priest's servant came, while the flesh was cooking, with a fleshhook of three teeth in his hand [eh?]. He struck it into a pan, or kettle, or cauldron, or pot; all that the fleshhook brought up the priest took for himself. It was a half-pound steak from Tesco's and cost £3. All in one you have a cleric and a greedy bugger.

And Eli blessed Elkanah and his wife, and said, 'The Lord give thee seed of this woman for the loan which is lent to the Lord at the bank rate of eleven per cent with interest.'

4. Then the Lord visited Hannah. She conceived three sons and two daughters.

5. Eli was very old on a zimmer, blessed by the Lord, but alas all night his two sons lay with two women on the steps of the tabernacle. Police arrested them for indecent exposure. At the trial they were sentenced to six months. The Judge sayeth, 'Have thee

anything to say?' And the sons answered, 'Ye will never stop fucking in Israel.'

The *Jewish Chronicle* said: 'Fornication on altar steps shock horror.' And Eli was cast down and said to his family, 'If one man sin against another, man will judge him, but if a man sin against God, what then?'

'He'll need a criminal lawyer and a bank loan,' said his family.

6. There came a man from God unto Eli and said, 'Telemessage. Did I not appear in thy home when you were in Egypt?'

'Yes,' sayeth Eli, 'it was in the lounge; you had a sherry.'

The man of the Lord sayeth, 'Did I give unto thine house offerings made by fire?'

'Well,' said Eli, 'actually, you burnt the kitchen down.'

The man of the Lord said, 'They that despise me shall be lightly esteemed – just lightly.'

Then bad news for Eli. 'Behold, the days come that I will cut off thine arm.'

'Are you a surgeon touting for work?' said Eli.

The man of God said, 'The Lord sayeth, "I will build for him a sure house." '

'Can you make it four bedrooms with a granny annexe,' sayeth Eli, 'and can it be freehold?'

Said the man of the Lord, 'There will come a time in thine house you will crouch to the Lord for a piece of silver and bread.'

'Can we have the silver first?' sayeth Eli.

7. The child Samuel ministered unto the Lord

before Eli. Samuel just got in first, the word of the Lord was precious in those days; there was no open vision, and there was no remote control, due to appalling lack of accommodation. Samuel slept on the temple steps and was covered in footprints. The Lord called Samuel, and he ran to Eli and said, 'I say, I say, I say, thou callest me.'

Eli said, 'No, go back to sleep.'

8. So he goeth, then the Lord called again, and He runneth to Eli and said, 'I say, I say, I say, thou callest me.'

And Eli sayeth, 'No, go back to sleep.'

So he goeth back, and the Lord called again, and Samuel runneth to Eli and said, 'I say, I say, I say, thou callest me.'

And Eli said, 'No, go back to sleep.'

And he goeth then. To keep the routine going, the Lord called Samuel again and Samuel runneth to Eli, 'I say, I say, I say, thou callest me,' said Samuel.

But Eli twigged it was the Lord calling, and said to Samuel, 'If He calleth again answer, "Speak, Lord".'

So back to sleep, and the Lord called on an extension, 'Samuel, Samuel.'

And Samuel sayeth, 'I say, I say, I say, speak, Lord.'

The Lord said unto Samuel, 'Behold, I will do a thing in Israel, at which both the ears of everyone that hear of it shall tingle.'

And, lo, the doctors of Israel were overwhelmed by people with tingling ears. And so Samuel was to be a prophet. 'I say, I say, I say, I'm going to be a prophet.'

And the word of Samuel came to all Israel, the word was Spazolikon.

9. Woe, the Israelites went to war with the Philistines, and the Philistines slaughtered the Israelites 7-0 and won the ark of the covenant. And when the supporters saw the score, a great wail went up, 'ARGGGGGH'. Eli heard the terrible ARGGGGGH and a supporter told him that the Israelites had lost and at that Eli fell backwards off his seat and his neck broke and he died. The ark of the Lord now belonged to the Philistines. And there were football riots, those that died now were smitten with haemorrhoids and screamed when they sitteth down. And Samuel judged Israel; he went on the circuit to Bethel, Gilgal and Mizpeh and judged in all those places.

10. His sentences went from a fine for swinging a cat in confined places to six months for doing it on the temple steps. When Samuel was old he set up his sons. In a blaze of nepotism he made them judges, but, woe, his sons walketh not in his ways; going for lucre, they took bribes. And the Lord spoke from a pillar of cloud on His new intercom: 'Did I not bring the Israelites out of Egypt, etc. Did I not get them across the Red Sea etc.?'

'Yes Lord etc.,' said Samuel. 'We know you did that for them, but what have you done for them lately?'

The Lord answered not but drew away on His pillar of cloud, then through His loud-hailer said, 'The people are calling for a king listen to them etc.'

So Samuel said unto the people of Israel, 'Go ye every

man unto his city,' and, lo, there be sixty-mile tailbacks of asses. The Lord and His pillar of cloud were hemmed in.

11. And there cometh a man called Saul, the Lord's choice in the coming election. Samuel took in Saul and said to the cook, 'Serve thou him.' And the cook took up the shoulder of lamb, and that which was upon it — fried onions and chips — and set it before Saul. 'Mint sauce?' said Samuel.

So did Saul eat with Samuel, the whole meal with VAT came to twelve pounds, fifty pence, service not included. And when they came down from the high place [they dined in a tree], Samuel communed with Saul up a ladder upon the top of the house. And they arose early and dropped off.

Samuel called Saul up the ladder again and Saul sayeth, 'Not bloody likely.'

Then Samuel took a vial of oil and poured it upon his head and kissed him. 'Oh, kinky eh?' said Saul.

12. Meantime, Saul's father's asses had gone missing. He putteth an entry in the *Jewish Chronicle*: small ads with a small reward of one shekel per donkey. And, lo, they brought back more than he had lost and had to pawn the fish knives. And the Lord spoke from inside a pay phone, 'Your father's asses hath been found,' and He sayeth, 'What shall I do for my son.'

'Tell him,' said Saul, 'the first thing is to help me get this oil off.'

The Lord telleth the father. 'Your son is well oiled.'

And the father sayeth, 'Pissed is he? Wait till he comes home.' And then the Lord's money runneth out.

13. Samuel sayeth unto Saul, 'Go thou to Tabor; there you will meet three men going up to God, one carrying three kids, one carrying three loaves of bread, one carrying a bottle of wine; it's Harrods' delivery service.'

Saul and his oil caught up with Harrods' delivery men; one gave him two loaves of bread. Saul said, 'These are white; have you any wholemeal?' Then the Bible says, 'God gave him [Saul] another heart', yet there is no previous incidence of heart trouble. The Bible goes on to say, 'and all those signs came to pass that day'; these must have been palpitations, dizziness and double vision. The chances are it was done on BUPA. Apparently, with the operation went the position of king. Samuel called the children of Israel to him and gave an inauguration talk: 'The Lord took you out of Egypt [Groans], He getteth you through the Red Sea [Groans].'

14. 'We know all about that,' said the children of Israel and Samuel fireth his speechwriter. And he was fearful of the mob and hid.

Samuel sayeth, 'This is no way to treat your king.'

And they sayeth, 'Where is he?'

And the Lord said, 'He hath hidden himself behind the stuff.'

A sniffer dog found it. And Saul came forth and they saw that, thanks to platform shoes, he was taller than they and sang, 'God save our gracious king, long live our noble king. God save our king.' And in graffiti they wrote, 'Have a ball with Saul. Walk tall with Saul. Saul has a vision to keep us in the first division.'

15. Samuel told the people the manner of the kingdom and wrote it in a book due for publication by Michael Joseph this autumn, *Israel On A Pound A Day*. It came to pass, Nahash the Ammonite came up to Jabesh. All the men of Jabesh said, 'Make a covenant with us.'

He said, [wait for it], 'Only if I can thrust out all your right eyes.'

And they said, 'You must be joking.'

And in the land the race of Israel calleth out for a leader like Moses, and they wept. And, behold, Saul came after the herd out of the field; and he had been treading in it. When they heard, the children of Israel cried – he was angry, the oil on his head started to bubble, he took a yoke of oxen and, using an MFI chainsaw, cut them into pieces.

'Feeling better?' said Samuel. 'Here, have one of these,' he said, passing him a Valium-soaked bagel.

16. Among the crowd was Nahash and his second-division Ammonites, shouting insults. 'Saul eats shell-fish and bacon.'

Lo, Saul's blood pressure goeth up to 160/100. On the morrow, Israelis in their first-division shirts attacketh the Ammonites and they scattered 'till none was left and they goeth not into extra time.

17. Saul said, 'I will speak with you, therefore stand still.'

And the Israelites said, 'It's all right Saul, we can hear when we're moving about.'

Then Samuel called unto the Lord, and the Lord sent

thunder and rain and play at Lord's was stopped. 'Putteth the covers on,' sayeth the Lord.

Saul counteth the children of Israel: there were three-hundred thousand women and thirty thousand men. 'Verily, the computer-dating service worketh not,' said Saul.

And Samuel spoke to all Israel – the talk was repeated that night. 'When Jacob came into Egypt, your fathers cried unto the Lord, we hardly got any sleep, and the Lord God brought you out of Egypt.'

The Israelites groaned.

18. And it came to pass, that the Philistines declareth war and advanced. When the men of Israel saw them, verily, then battle goeth, they hideth themselves in caves, in thickets, in rocks, in high places, in cupboards, under floorboards, behind trees, under beds, in cellars, in sheds, in stables, in toilets, in drainpipes, under blankets, down coalholes, in attics, behind mothers-in-law.

19. From his new CD Saul blew the trumpet throughout Israel; it was to tell them of the victory of Jonathan, his son, and him against the Philistines who had been sorely smote.

And Saul said, 'Bring hither a peace burnt offering.'

And he offered the burnt offering, and as there were no takers he ate the burnt offering; it was a three-course burnt offering, finishing with rice pudding and jam.

Then Samuel arrived by fast zimmer and he said to Saul, 'What hast thou done?'

'I hast not done anything,' said Saul. 'Why, can you smell something?'

Samuel said, 'Did thou smite the Philistines?'

'Yea,' said Saul, 'they are one mass of smites.'

20. Samuel and Saul called on the Lord for the victory, but He had gone out for a spin in His pillar of cloud. And, woe, the Philistines were gathering to strike again and they camped at Michmash, a suburb of Israel with low-price housing and a neighbourhood watch. Now there crept up on the Philistines, Saul's son Jonathan, and the Philistines spotted Jonathan: 'Come up, we will show thee a thing.'

But before the Philistine could show his thing, Jonathan smote, slew and slaughtered them and the Philistines were sore afraid, their trousers were full of it, but, thanks to dry cleaning, the Philistines attacked again.

21. And the Lord spoke to Saul: 'Attack thou all the uncircumcised ones.'

'But, Lord,' sayeth Saul, 'that meanest we'll have to keep looking up their trouser legs.' The Lord driveth away on a diesel-powered pillar of cloud and, lo, the uncircumcised Philistines fled, clutching their willies. And Saul said, 'Let us go after the Philistines by night and spoil them [eh?].' So they did and by dawn most of the Philistines had been spoilt [eh?]. And the Lord spoke from a bolt of lightning with singed eyebrows. He was well pleased for now the uncircumcised ones of the Philistines were queuing up for the operation.

22. And the war against the Philistines was all the days of Saul. When Saul saw any strong man or valiant man, he took him into him, and there was gossip. The

Lord spoke to Samuel: 'Saul hath not kept my commandments.'

It grieved Samuel, he cried unto the Lord all night. But He heareth him not, thanks to double glazing. Samuel said to Saul, 'What meaneth this bleating of sheep and lowing of oxen in my ears?'

Saul said, 'It means you can hear sheep and oxen. They are being saved for steak and kidney pie with a side salad for the Lord.'

'Is it a burnt offering?' said Samuel.

'No,' said Saul, 'just grilled.'

The Lord was wrath for He liketh not steak and kidney pie, but chicken livers and blintzes, and He striketh the steak and kidney pie with lightning and rain to fall on the side salad.

23. Now it came to pass, that Samuel had captured king Agag and said to him, 'As thy sword hath made women childless, so shall thy mother be childless.' And Samuel hewed Agag in pieces before the Lord. [Actually, it was murder, but in the Bible you got away with it.] And Samuel thanked the Lord for not turning him in.

24. Samuel never went to Saul any more, mainly because he was dead. The Lord said unto Samuel, 'How long wilt thou mourn for Saul?'

And Samuel said, 'About twenty minutes a day for a week.'

And, lo, again the Philistines sought battle, among them Goliath who stood six cubits and a span. When he had to think his brain hurt, and he calleth to the Israelites, 'Der-I challenge-der-anybody to-der-fight me.' Having to speak so many words tired him and he had to sit down.

Then, from out of the Israelite Army, stepped a young Israelite with three 'O' and six 'A' levels named David. 'I will fight thee,' he challenged Goliath.

25. And the Philistines said to David, 'Come to me, and I will give thy flesh unto the fowls of the air, and to the beasts of the field.'

And David said, 'Sticks and stones can hurt my bones but bad words never hurt me.'

The bookies gave 100-1 David, and Goliath 7-to-4 on. The great oaf of a giant drew his sword and swished it round his head, slicing his ear off. 'Oh,' he said, 'I can't hear so good.'

David took up his sling, put a rock in it and hurled it at Goliath. It struck him between his eyes, he reeled backward, he reeled forward, he reeled upright, then crashed to the ground.

David rushed forward, drew Goliath's sword and struck off his head.

'Now, come home, son,' said David's mother. 'I've got some nice chicken livers for your supper.'

And women came out of the city, dancing and playing top ten Israelite hits, and they danced around David. Saul, who was not as dead as we thought — 'Saul still alive' says *Jewish Chronicle* — was jealous for whereas he had killed thousands, David had only killed one.

26. Saul was wrath, he swingeth the cat round and round his head and let it fly out the window. An evil spirit like Jeyes Fluid came upon Saul; he prophesied in

the middle of the house, all over the carpet, his mother made him clean it up. David played with his hand as at other times [eh?]. And then, [get this], Saul removed him from him; and he went out and came in before the people?!? Now Michal, Saul's daughter, loved David, therefore Saul said, 'Thou shalt this day be my son-in-law, but you'll have to stop carrying that giant's head around. I want not a dowry, instead I want a hundred foreskins of the Philistines.'

David arose, went and slew two hundred Philistines and David brought their foreskins and counted them out in front of Saul.

Saul said, 'There be twice the amount I wanted.'

'Use them as spares,' said David.

27. So Saul gave David Michal to wife. And on their wedding night there was Jewish foreplay: twenty minutes' begging and a blank cheque.

It came to pass that Saul, after he cashed the cheque, swore to kill David, but Michal let David down through a window into a water butt. Then, using a bolster and goats' hair, she made a dummy in David's bed. Saul burst in the room, but Michal cleaned it up. Then Saul, with a cry of 'Die David', stuck his sword into the bolster, but no blood cometh out. 'He bleedeth not,' said Saul.

'He's anaemic,' said Michal.

'Why has thou deceived me with goats' hair?' said Saul.

'It was cheaper than mink,' sayeth Michal.

David fled to the YMCA and the Lord God went before him in a pillar of cloud after its thousand-mile service. And the Lord was with David on flexitime.

28A. David stripped off his clothes and prophesied before Samuel, and lay down naked, and prophesied he'd get bronchitis, which came to pass.

David said to Jonathan, 'Why does thy father seekest my life?'

Jonathan said, 'My father will do nothing either great or small, but that he will show it to me: and why should my father hide this thing from me?'

'Never mind all the crap,' said David, 'your father wants me dead.'

And David arose out of a place towards the south and fell on his face before the Lord in a north-easterly direction, then bowed south-south-west; all wasted as God was due east. Then Jonathan and David kissed one another, until David exceeded [Eh?].

28B. And Jonathan returned to the city to find the FT Index up twenty-seven points. Meanwhile, David seeketh shelter with a priest, Ahimelech. 'I am of hunger,' said David; 'give me five loaves of bread, they should last me 'till Thursday.'

The priest said, 'I have no common bread, only hallowed bread for men who have kept themselves from women.'

My God, I'm going to starve, thought David. 'Nay, I haven't touched a woman,' said David.

'Then how do you do it?' said the priest.

He giveth David bread saying, 'It is fresh, but best eaten before the 15th.'

And so David eateth the bread with low-fat spread.

29. And David arose, and his bottle goeth and he

fled and went to Achish, the king of Gath, who was suspicious of David as he telleth him he was a humble travelling trombonist. But the king sayeth, 'This bloke is barmy; he sayest he is a trombonist, but hath none.'

30. And David was sore afraid of the king of Gath. He went on acting mad, playing an invisible trombone. He was asked to leave, and he escaped to the cave Adullam. And everyone that was in distress, and everyone in debt, and everyone wanted for house breaking, gathered themselves unto him; and he became their captain, he was still not very well. Before the police came David left and asked refuge with the king of Moab. And he let him dwell in the hold, and the prophet Gad said unto David, 'Abide not in the hold, you'll suffocate; flee ye to Judah, take the "B" roads to avoid tollgates.'

31. Saul had Ahimelech taken prisoner. 'Why did you give him bread?' he said.

'He was hungry,' said the priest.

'Don't give me that crap,' said Saul, so the priest didn't give him that crap. Saul had half an hour to kill, so he killed the priest; it took days to get the stain out of the carpet.

And they told David of Saul's deed. David calleth to the Lord for vengeance, and the Lord said bring it up at the next court of petty sessions. Then they told David, 'Behold, the Philistines are fighting against Keilah, and they have robbed the threshing room floor, nobody has anything to stand on.' The Lord spoke from a barrel of lug worms. 'Arise, go and smite the Philistines but keep damage to property to a minimum.'

And David smoted the Philistines, not one remained without smote marks.

32. It seemed these days as if the Lord God was on anybody's side. Here He was supporting Saul, David and Samuel. When Saul knew David was in town he said, 'God hath delivered him to me [He's now on Saul's side]; he is trapped, coming into a town that hath gates and bars.'

In fact, at the time David was in one of the bars, drinking a crisp young dry white Hebron wine selling at £2.50 a bottle. Then, after a few, he got up off the floor and said, 'O Lord of Israel [He's on David's side now], will Saul come down here?'

And the Lord said, 'He will come down here.'

Then David and his men runneth like fuck and hideth in the wilderness of Ziph.

33. Following a trail of empty bottles of crisp young dry white Hebron wine, Jonathan found David and his men on their last bottle, and for David strengthened his hand in God [still on David's side]. The Lord appeared in a snow cloud and His teeth chattereth. There came Ziphites, traditional sneaks and shits, who told Saul, 'David hideth in the wilderness of Ziph, which is on the south side of Jeshimon.' [Actually, it was on the north side.] So Saul said of these sneaky lot of shits, 'Blessed be ye of the Lord.' [Now on Saul's side.]

34. Saul and the Ziphite sneaky lot of shits hurried to trap David in the wilderness of Ziph, but David and his men were hiding in the wilderness of Maon, the land around ripe for development; indeed, David and his men developed a liking for women and wine, the

lower clan birds and beer. Then Saul had news that the Philistines were sacking his palace; they had also sacked the cook and the butler. David thanked the Lord for his lucky escape. The Lord heard him not as His hearing had faileth.

35. Now Saul came searching for David but David hideth in a cave; and Saul went in to cover his feet [eh?]. David arose from the lotus position, and [here it comes] cut off the skirt of Saul's robe privily. Why Saul was in drag has never really been answered. It came to pass, David's heart smote him for having ruined Saul's dress. It was red with a split skirt worn with black stockings and white stiletto shoes. Saul looked lovely in it. Then Saul, furious, rose up out of the cave and went on his way somewhere.

David ran after Saul, and said, 'My Lord the king.' David stooped with his face to the earth, bowed low.

'Very good,' said Saul, 'but I'm not there, I'm here behind you.'

David said, 'I cut off thy skirt, but killed ye not.' Then he speaketh gobbledegook! 'After whom is the king of Israel come out? After whom dost thou pursue? After a dead dog, after a flea.'

Saul sayeth, 'I knoweth nothing about a dead dog or a flea; has the owner been informed?'

And David goeth on with the gobbledegooketh: 'For if a man find his enemy, wherefore so shall that he upon me then.'

Saul listened.

And the Lord sayeth, 'Woe, I cannot take any more

of this,' and He departeth on a maroon-endowed pillar of cloud.

36. Samuel died, and they gathered together to hear the will read. He left it all to the Israelite home for fallen ladies; he himself had fallen for one or two. His wife put an obit in the *Jewish Chronicle*. 'Just say Samuel is dead,' she said.

The man said, 'You're allowed six words.'

'All right,' she said, 'say, "Samuel is dead, Volvo for sale."'

37. There was a man in Maon, he had three thousand sheep and a thousand goats; it was everywhere. He was shearing his sheep in Carmel, a wholesale knitwear shop like Harrods without the Arabs. The man's name was Nabal, one of Lloyd's Names; that's why he never slept. His wife was Abigail: she was beautiful, on a bad day 36-28-36, on a good 40-30-36. She was of a lovely disposition and would do it anytime. Nabal was churlish – sometimes he would churl night and day. He paid his shearers two shekels and all the wool they could eat. David sent his shearers at one shekel an hour. Nabal told them to pisseth off. David was wrath, he and his men put on their swords, girded their loins, also girded their teeth and ears, then set off for a jolly good afternoon's killing. And they met Abigail, coming the other way.

'Oh, hello,' said David. 'We're just off to kill your husband.'

Abigail threw herself at David's feet and missed.

38. And she sayeth, 'My lord, I pray thee, pity my

husband and Sheepshearing PLC, folly is with him, and I sawest not your shekel-an-hour shearers come. Now therefore, my lord, as the Lord liveth, He has withholden thee from coming to shed blood with thine own hand. Now let thine enemies, and they that seek evil to my lord, be as Nahal.'

'What a load of crap,' sayeth David. 'Take this woman's measurements.'

And, lo, she was 40-30-36.

David looked kindly on her measurements and said to Abigail, 'Blessed be the Lord God of Israel, who sent thee to me,' and he gave them a squeeze. 'Tell your husband I will not put in a takeover bid for Sheepshearing PLC; surely there had not been left unto Nabal any that pisseth against the wall.'

Abigail then made an offering to him: two hundred loaves; two bottles of wine; five sheep, oven-ready.

'Thank you,' said Abigail, 'that will be eighty nine shekels fifty.'

'Visa?' said David. Then David proposed to Abigail on bended knees, hers.

39. She returned to Nabal, and he putteth on a feast; he eateth all fatty things, his cholesterol was 10.3. And it came to pass the Lord smote Nabal and he died. Good old God. Abigail was free to marry David. She rode upon an ass with five damsels, the ass could hardly move but a touch of pepper on the ass's bum and he was away. Now those little shits the Ziphites came and told Saul where David was. He hideth himself in the hill of Hachilah. 'It's on the B2089.' So Saul took three thousand men.

40. And Saul pitched his tent on the side of Mount Hachilah, and it slid down the side. But David hath fled into the wilderness and was in a cave doing it to Abigail. He getteth off, giveth it a quick shake, then he and his men goeth to find Saul, and they found him asleep in a trench. And Abishai said to David, 'God hath delivered Saul into thine hands: let me smite him with a spear and pin him to the earth; I play darts so I'm pretty good at it.'

David said, 'Nay, the Lord shall smite him, He's very good at this; it's usually a heart attack.'

Then they saw Saul's battle spear by his side. 'Take that,' said David. 'It'll do well at a boot sale.'

Then David went to the top of a hill; a great space being between them. And he cried to the people, 'You're too bloody far.'

And the people said, 'We can't hear a word.'

But Saul heard him and said, 'Is that the voice of David?'

'Yes,' said David, 'it is mine; I always use it.'

41. The two-faced pair now went into gobbledegook talk. David said, 'Wherefore doth my lord thus pursue me with a bloody great spear?'

Then Saul said, 'I have sinned: I will no more do thee harm. Can I have my spear back?'

David said, 'I will not stretch forth my hand against the Lord's anointed.'

Saul said, 'Blessed be thou.'

So David went his way, swearing vengeance and Saul returned to his place, swearing vengeance. And the Lord God blessed them and left to hurl fire and brimstone on a city.

42. And David said, 'I will now perish one day by that bastard Saul: I shall flee to the land of the Philistines and their team West Ham.' So after a quick begatting with Abigail, he set off and he dwelleth with Achish. It was full board, three shekels 50 pence a week.

And the Lord spoke to David from a burning bush wearing an asbestos suit: 'I am the Lord God,' He sayeth.

And David said, 'Of course you are.'

43. Now those shits the Ziphites told Saul that David had fled to Gath. Then Achish put the rent up, so David and his yobboes invaded the Geshurites, the Gezrites, and the Amalekites; they smote the land, and left neither man nor woman alive.

And the Philistines, now armed with spear-throwing chariots, marched on Israel. And Achish said, 'David, thou shall come to battle with me – I will make you keeper of mine head for ever.'

David said, 'OK, but can you keep it for the time being?'

And Saul saw the host of the Philistines and his bottle goeth, and Saul calleth out to the Lord, but owing to freak weather conditions, He heareth him not. So Saul goeth to the witch of Endor; even though the waiting room was full, she saw him first. She goeth into a trance and told him it was ten shekels an hour in cash. Then she said, 'I see a vision.'

44. 'Is it a good picture?' said Saul.

'I see an old man; he is covered in a blanket.'

'He must be cold,' said Saul. When he saw it was the

late Samuel, Saul stooped with his face to the ground, and bowed.

'It's too late for that,' said Samuel; 'I'm dead.'

'You've cost me ten shekels,' said Saul.

Samuel shook his head, turned to the witch of Endor and said, 'You know my fee, it's fifty.'

'It was a special offer,' said the witch.

After he had sung 'My Yiddisher Mama', Samuel told Saul that the Philistines would outsmite the Israelites.

45. Then Saul fell, face down, straight away all along the earth and squashed them. There was no strength in him; for he had eaten no bread all the day, only a Yorkie bar. And the witch baked unleavened bread, then gave it in great lumps to Saul and his yobboes and they did eat. They rose up and went away with indigestion.

46. The Philistines lay ready for battle. They said, 'Who are these Hebrews?'

Achish said, 'This is David, and he's looking after my head.'

The Philistine princes said, 'Send him away, he's circumcised.' So because of a clipped willy he was sent back. When David and his yobs returned to Ziklag, to his horror he found a tribe called the Bailiffs had been and taken everything: the furniture – even the wives. And all David's yobs cried because their furniture was on HP. David was distressed as the people spake of stoning him. One or two rocks bounced off his heart, but that was all.

47. David called on the Lord, who spoke to him from

a burning bush that goeth out. David prostrated himself face down on the earth. A chariot ran over him. 'Lord,' said David, 'should I pursue the Bailiffs?'

'Surely,' said the Lord, trying to kick-start the bush, 'if thy furniture be on HP, I will help you smite the Bailiffs.'

Then David took all the HP agreements and placed them in his underpants where no human had ever set forth. At dawn, after a hard night's sleeping, David and his men set off after the Bailiffs. There is in the desert the oasis of Barloks. Sure, David and his men caught the Bailiffs by the Barlocks; there cometh screams of 'Let go.' David smote them from twilight (about 6.30) into the evening of the next day (about 4 o'clock) with only one break for lunch. Not a Bailiff escaped except four hundred young men on camels who fled looking for oil. David saveth his wife Abigail, whom he took to a cave where he transferreth the HP agreements from his underpants into Abigail's knickers.

⚜ CHAPTER XII ⚜

IT CAME TO PASS, a man came with ragged clothes all rent and David sayeth, 'Art thou looking for a tailor?' The man fell on his face before David. 'Upsydaisy,' said David.

'I'm sorry,' said the man, 'I don't know how to up a daisy.' He told David, 'Saul and Jonathan are dead.'

'How do you know?' said David.

'Because they buried them,' said the prostrate man.

2. ''Twas in the midst of battle, Saul sayeth to me, "Who art thou?" and I said, "I'm an Amalekite." He said, "Pray, stand on me and slay me; the battle is lost." I said, "I hardly know you," but he pressed me hard, so I slew him and I took the crown from his head. I have brought it to you, my Lord; it's hallmarked 14 carat gold.'

Then David rent his clothes, he beateth his breast, breaking three ribs. He mourned the heroes of the house of Israel that had fallen by the sword; some of the heroes had fallen running away. Then David said unto the Amalekite, 'How dare you kill Saul, the Lord's anointed?'

'He didn't want to be captured by the uncircumcised ones and be exposed,' said the Amalekite.

David called his young soldiers, 'Go near, and fall upon him.' And he smote him so hard that he died.

'Is that all, sir?' said the soldier.

'Yes,' said David. 'O Israel, how are the mighty fallen. Tell it not in Gath, publish it not in the *Jewish Chronicle* lest the daughters of the uncircumcised laugh.'

3. David asked the Lord, 'Shall I go up to Hebron?'

The Lord said, 'No, go down to Hebron for that's where it is.' So David went down thither, and he thithered all the way to Hebron; there he met the men that buried Saul.

David said, 'The Lord's blessing on you who buried him.'

'Well,' said the men, 'in his condition it seemed the best thing to do.'

Abner, the son of Ner, took Ishbosheth and took him to Mahanaim; and that got rid of them. And David ruled in Hebron over Judah with a rod of iron; when that got too heavy he used a wooden one.

4. Then Abner son of Ner took the servants of Ishbosheth, and went out from Mahanaim to Gibeon, and that got rid of them. Joab and the servants went and sat by the pool of Gibeon. On the other side sat Abner and his servants. Abner said, 'Let the young men now arise, and play before us.' And the servants arose and started to play at killing each other. Abner's were beaten. The Lord appeared in a cloud and sayeth, 'Tsu, Tsu.' Why the bloodshed occurred the Bible explaineth not, save that the spot where the killing took place was 'Wherefore that place was called Helkathhazzurim.' To announce peace on the land Joab blew a great blast on the

trumpet, and got a lump in his groin. Meantime, Abner and what were left of his men walked all night through the plain, and passed over the Jordan, through Bithron, to Mahanaim and that got rid of them.

5. There was a war between the house of Saul and the house of David, but David waxed stronger and stronger and the house of Saul waxed weaker and weaker. Tiles fell off the roof, the water tank burst and ruined the lounge – there was dry rot in the joists. And Saul moveth in with his mother-in-law, who had a face like a chicken's bum. The war continued, and Abner made himself strong for the house of Saul. He shored up the roof timbers, replastered the lounge and put in a shower; he did it for a knockdown price. When Saul heard it, he knocked him down. Then Saul attacked David: he showed him a photograph of his mother-in-law and David fled the field shouting 'Unfair!' Saul had a concubine named Rizpah.

6. One day – quite a nice day, some cloud, 30 degrees Centigrade with a forecast of rain – Ishbosheth said to Abner, 'Why hast thou gone in unto my father's concubine?'

Abner was wrath. 'I've never ever been in unto a concubine. I, who replastered your father's kitchen.'

7. Meantime, David sent messengers to Ishbosheth, saying, 'Deliver me my wife Michal, which I espoused to me for a hundred foreskins of the Philistines.'

Ishbosheth took Michal and the dowry, a bag of one hundred foreskins. But now, aha, Abner is going to change sides, he goeth to David and sweareth loyalty at the going rate of ten shekels an hour, so David putteth on a feast:

MENU

Brown Windsor Soup

Roast Beef and Two Veg

Apple Pie and Custard

8. And Abner said, 'I will arise and go, and draw all Israel unto my Lord.'

Then arrived Michal with the bag of foreskins. David counted them. 'There's one missing,' he said.

'I know,' said Michal, 'I gave it as a tip to a waiter.'

Then arrived Joab with his troop and brought in a great spoil, David took fifty spoils for himself giving the rest to Joab. When Joab heard that Abner had been here he waxed wrath, pulse 81, blood pressure 180/100. 'Knowest Abner came to deceive thee, to know thou going out and coming in, and to know all that thou doest.'

'I haven't been out or in and the only thing I've been doing is Michal.'

Joab stamped on a burning coal and set off hotfoot after Abner. When he found him he smote him under the fifth rib and he died. It's a miracle anyone is left alive in the Bible. We'll press on 'till the next death via the fifth rib.

9. And they buried Abner; it was the best thing really. And all the people wept over him, he was soaked. And the Beerothites fled to Gittaim and were sojourners there unto this day [Reuter]. Now Jonathan, Saul's son, had a son who was lame; it happened when his nurse took him up,

and fled, and as she made haste she dropped the boy under her ass. His name was Mephibosheth. Now when Saul's son heard that Abner was dead his hands went feeble and he couldn't scratch his parts any more. As mourning for Abner, David foreswore no food would pass his lips 'till the sun set. The sun went behind a cloud immediately, and David started a seven-course dinner. 'But', sayeth the punters, 'it hath not set; it is behind a cloud.'

'That's near enough for me,' sayeth David.

10. It came to pass, Rechab and his brother Baanah went to the house of Ishbosheth, who lay on his bed doing Swedish relief massage. The brothers entered the house as though they were fetching wheat, then they smote Ishbosheth under his [guess where?] fifth rib, then beheaded him. They took it to David saying, 'Surprise, surprise', and showed him the head. David was wrath, in rage he stampeth his foot and fractured his ankle. He commanded his men, who slew the brothers badly, it was two less in the Bible story. Ishbosheth's head they buried in a hat box, size six and seven-eighths. At this point in the Bible there are no recent sightings of the Lord God or His pillar of cloud.

11. Then came the tribes of Israel, among them there were many overdrafts, and they spoke unto David saying, 'We are thy bone and thy flesh.'

'I wondered where it was,' said David.

And they said, 'The Lord hath said unto thee, thou shall feed my people.'

'Yes,' said David, 'but it will have to be self-service.' David ruled and grew great, eighteen stone, and the

Lord God of hosts was with him at eleven stone ten pounds. Now David took ten more concubines and wives, and had to have the bed reinforced. As David was now king he spent his time running between the bed and the throne, and was on testosterone tablets. Then God anointed David; it was all over his forehead.

12. When the Philistines knew that David had been anointed king, they came up to seek him. David went down in the hold to hide, taking with him six concubines and a bed. In between David said to the Lord, 'Should I take on the Philistines?'

God said, 'Go thou to the mulberry trees, when thou hearest sounds on the tops of the trees, strike.'

David heard the Philistine Army up the mulberry trees, he droppeth it down and slayed them all by the fifth rib. Then David set the ark on a new cart, and he played before the Lord harps, bells, timbrels, drums, cornets and cymbals.

The Lord sent an archangel down to say, 'You noisy bastard.'

The record still went to No. 2 in the Israelite charts. On the journey Uzzah, the driver, put forth his hand to hold the ark still, for the oxen shook it; it was the first time an ox and a man had shaken hands in the Bible.

13. For touching the ark the Lord was angered against Uzzah, so He smote him and there he died. David was displeased with God; he spat in a rage and in a rage it went down his chin. Because of what happened to Uzzah, David was feared to touch the ark, but moved it later wearing anti-Aids rubber gloves into the house

of a congenital idiot called Obededom, a name hard to say unless clutching the scrotum. If you clutched his scrotum, he could say it. With a post-dated cheque David laid on a dinner until the manager asked him to get off. Then David with rouged cheeks and a touch of lipstick danced before the Lord, naked except for a knee-length ephod and a St Michael brand jockstrap.

14. And all Israel feared to touch the ark, they brought it up on a plank of wood, with shouting drums and trumpets, they were all fined for disturbing the peace and agonised shouts of Obededom! From a window Michal, Saul's daughter, saw king David leaping dancing and mincing before the Lord, and she despised him in her heart, also in her lungs, kidneys and liver. And David offered a burnt offering – three pieces of toast; he blessed the people and all those who had lost teeth eating his toast.

15. Then David took off his make-up and went home. Michal greeted him. 'How glorious you were today, who uncovered himself in the eyes of the people, as one of the vain fellows shamelessly uncovereth himself.'

16. God said to David, 'Can you build me a house? I have not dwelt in any house since coming out of Egypt.'

'You've got your pillar of cloud,' said David.

So David built God a house. He put it on the market at twenty thousand shekels but God knocked him down. He agreed fifteen thousand, but still the Lord complaineth about the wallpaper in the kitchen.

17. And there was peace in the land. So putting his

concubines on hold, David attacked and smote the poor
bloody Philistines who were bottom of the league table,
having just lost to Swindon. He then smote the king of
Zobah as he was on his way to the Euphrates to recover
his border, who had done a moonlight with the rent.
Then king Zobah gave spoils of victory, vessels of gold,
silver and brass. David prostrated himself and dedicated
the brass vessels to the Lord; the silver and gold went to
auction.

18. One day, in between concubines, he said, 'Are
there any relatives of Saul left?'

'Yes, but no thanks to you,' said Ziba, the butler.

He brought before David the lame boy Mephibosheth,
who fell on his face before David.

'There's no need to do reverence to me,' said David.

'I wasn't,' said the boy, 'I fell over.'

And David said unto Ziba, 'Thou shalt look after this
boy; you will do his cooking, cleaning his launder.' And
Ziba wished to God he'd never brought the little bastard in.

19. It came to pass, the king of Ammon snuffed it,
and Hanun, his son, reigned instead. David sent servants
to commiserate, but Hanun, the little creep, suspected
them of spying. He took David's servants, shaved off
one half of their beards, cut off their garments in the
middle, exposing all the wedding tackle and buttocks;
on their return home some women applauded them and
offered marriage. When they told David he cried, 'The
suspicious bastard.' And yes! He went a-smoting Ammonites and when Hanun saw David charging in his chariot
with the meter on thirty shekels fifty, he crappeth him

and shouted 'Fainits'. 'Sod "fainits",' said David, driving his chariot on Hanun's chest. He leant out, shaved off half his head, cut his clothes, exposing his willy and bum. 'There,' said David, 'see how you like it.'

'Slightly shorter,' said Hanun. And David drove on, shaving the Ammonites' beards, exposing their willies and bums. It was too much for them and they threw down the arms and legs. Then David paid the chariot driver and went home.

20. On the way back he saw a woman washing herself. David estimated 40-28-38; she was Bathsheba. She was beautiful using Oil of Ulay, and with begging and a blank cheque she was soon begatting with David. One day David sent for Uriah. 'Go down to thy house and wash your feet; here, take this scrubbing brush and the OdorEaters.' Uriah departed out of the king's house, and there followed him a mess of meat from the king. Uriah turned and got it all in the face. And oh, how David laughed. Uriah was wrath and did not wash his feet, and David was angry; he sent Uriah to battle where the fighting was most dangerous. And, in time, Uriah was attacking a city wall and a woman above dropped a millstone on his nut and killed him. How David laughed.

21. When Uriah's wife heard of his death she mourned him and cashed in his life policy. King David fetched her to his home; he did twenty minutes' begging, gave her a blank cheque and started begatting. But the thing that David had done displeased the Lord.

The Lord spoke out of a steam cloud. 'David, thou naughty, naughty king, I will take thy wives before thine eyes and give them unto your neighbour, and he shall lie with thy wives in the sun. For thou didst it secretly: but I will do this thing before all Israel, and before the sun.'

'It ought to go down well,' said David.

22. Meantime, Joab was fighting against Rabbah of Ammon and had taken the city. He sent for David, 'You'll have to come and help, I've got tennis elbow and can't fight; I'd also like my wages revived.' So David put on his armoured jockstrap and marched on the city, let go smote after smote; he was doing nearly fifty smotes an hour and the city fell. Fortunately, it fell away from him, crushing the National Provincial office. He took their king's crown and placed it on his own head, but it slid over his eyes. The crown was of gold set with precious stones. David had it valued; at the sale he put a reserve on it of a thousand talents.

23. He then brought forth the people of the city; he put them under saws, under harrows of iron, and made them pass through a brick kiln. It was time king David saw a psychiatrist. Now another looney, Amnon, son of David, had the hots for his sister Tamar. His friend, Jonadab, told him how to get her, 'Make thyself sick.' It was all over the pillow. And Tamar came and Amnon grabbed her and married her from the waist down. Tamar was woe; she put ashes on her head, and rent her garments, and she went on crying. And Absalom her brother sayeth, 'Had a good shag?'

24. And Tamar crieth, 'He rapeth me.' And she showed Absalom the blank cheque. She cried bitterly as she filled in the amount: a hundred thousand shekels.

CHAPTER XII

'That should stop him fucking for some time,' said Absalom, but he hated Amnon for what and who he had done and swore vengeance. He inviteth all the king's sons to a fork supper, and as they eateth potato salad with basil, he instructeth his servant Addit, 'When Amnon is merry on the two-shekel bottle of wine kill him.' So Addit plunged the carving knife into Amnon's back and he falleth forward into the Black Forest Gateau. At this all the king's sons got on their mules and ran like hell for safety. When David heard the news he stopped doing it, he and his servant wept very sore, and they useth Ponds' Cold Cream.

25. Meanwhile, Absalom fled as fast as his ass would go. The king said to Joab, 'Go, bring Absalom back, but let him not see my face.' It was the nose job. Absalom came back, but did not see David's face, or the nose job. Absalom polled* his head every year; he polled his head because the hair was heavy, so he polled it. He weighed the hair of his head at two hundred shekels king's weight, which wasn't much for making thyself bald. He dwelt on two more years in Jerusalem, but saw not the king's face; occasionally, he saw a leg. Absalom inviteth Joab to supper, but he cometh not, so Absalom goeth to Joab's field of barley and set fire to it. Then Joab came to supper asking, 'Why hast thou set fire to my field?'

'I was cold,' said Absalom, and Joab hitteth him straight in the conk and it spreadeth around his face and unto his ear.

* Shaved

141

26. So Joab sent back to David, who sayeth, 'I see you've had a nose job too.' Then came Absalom; by now David's nose job was better and he kissed Absalom; hello sailor. Now Absalom swore he would dethrone David, and he went among the people telling lies about David, only stopping to kiss the men. And a messenger came to David saying the people were massing behind Absalom because he was so lovely; bald but lovely.

27. David hastened to flee the palace, he changeth the locks, he left behind ten worn-out concubines on recharge; outside he had a chariot waiting with the horses running and he fled and tarried in a place far off – it might have been Lewisham. And Ittai the physician came and said, 'The nose job wasn't so good.'

'I'll sue BUPA,' said David.

Ittai sayeth, 'As the Lord liveth, and as my lord the king liveth, surely in what place my lord the king shall be, whether in death or life, even there also will thy servant be.'

'What the bloody hell are you talking about?' said David.

And Ittai burst into tears. 'You're so cruel,' he said.

And David said, 'Go and pass over.' So he passed over, then the people passed over, and the king passed over, everyone else passed over. What they were passing over, the Bible doesn't say.

28. The king said to Zadok [Who?], 'Take back the ark of God into the City, and pray I will find favour with the Lord. I will tarry in the plain in the wilderness, until there come word from you to certify me.'

CHAPTER XII

So he tarried in the wilderness, he tarried here, he tarried against a tree, a wall and out the window. Zadok [Who??] carried the ark to Jerusalem and he tarried there. And David went up Mount Olivet and he wept as he went, because he could not afford the ski lift. When he got to the top he tarried again, and there drew nigh Hushai the Archite, a *Daily Telegraph* clue; his coat was rent and he had earth on his head, most people have hair but he had earth.

29. David said, 'Why goest thee in ragged raiments?'

And when Hushai the Archite said, 'It's something to do with the shortage of money,' David said, 'If thou passeth on with me, then thou shall be a burden unto me.'

'I don't know what the bloody hell you are talking about,' said Hushai the Archite.

'Neither do I,' said David.

When David was a little over the top of the hill, Ziba [Who?] met him with asses, two hundred loaves of bread, and a bottle of wine.

'Is this what you call room service?' said David.

Ziba said, 'The asses be for the king's household to ride on; the bread is for the young men to eat; the wine is to get pissed on.'

David travelled on his ass to Bahumrim on the M20. As he arriveth, a nut called Shimei cursed him. 'Bugger off,' he crieth and hurled stones. 'You bastard,' said Shimei, 'one of your concubines is my daughter and she said you used appliances on her.'

'It's only a feather duster,' said David, as the stones bounced off his head.

Then said Abishai, 'Why should you take all this, let me go and take off his head.' So he went and cut it off. At once the stoning stopped and so did Shimei.

30. It came to pass, Hushai the Archite, David's friend, came unto Absalom and sang, 'God save our gracious king, long live our gracious king, God save our king, send him victorious, happy and glorious, long to reign over us, God save our king.'

'Don't give up your day job,' said Absalom.

Then Ahithophel, another crossword clue, took Absalom to one side and joined him there: 'Go thou unto thy father's concubines and restart them.'

31. So Absalom goeth and giveth each concubine a thousand-mile service. For him to rest in, they spread a tent on top of the house, he goeth in, he sneezeth and he goeth through the roof. Then said Absalom to Ahithophel, 'Give counsel as to what I should do.'

'First,' said Ahithophel, 'get up off the floor, then have the roof mended.' Now Ahithophel counselled in those days like an oracle of God so his counsel was both with David and Absalom, the two-faced bastard.

32. Meanwhile, the concubines were crying for David; they were missing the whips and the leather gear. Now Ahithophel, asshole that he was, said to Absalom, 'Let me take a thousand men and pursue David to death by the fifth rib.' But Hushai the Archite warned Absalom, 'David is a man of war and has a mighty army — he won't be a pushover.' So Absalom

stayed Ahithophel's hand, knee and foot. Hushai the Archite sent warning to David: 'Stop not to tarry anywhere, but speedily pass over. Best wishes, Hushai.' Now Jonathan and Ahimaaz stayed by Enrogel [Enrogel! The ointment that masters piles]. Absalom was seeking them out, but they found a well and they went down and hideth. They cometh up next morning soaked, with pneumonia, and they goeth to David and warneth him that Absalom wants to kill his fifth rib. David goeth white as a sheet and let one go, then at speed David and his removal vans crossed the River Jordan, taking everything, including Weetabix. There came to pass a mighty Third World battle twixt David and Absalom, David outsmoted Absalom by a hundred smotes to ten, and Absalom fled on a mule.

33. But as he rode under the thick boughs of a great oak and his head caught in a fork, the mule went away leaving him hanging there, where Joab slew him. They cast his body in a pit and laid a heap of stones on him; he'd never get out. Then Joab gave a blast on the trumpet and his trousers falleth down, showing a healthy balance. David sat by the city gates, and a watchman went up on to the roof. He lifted up his eyes and fell off, landing at the feet of David. 'What's happening?' said David.

'I don't know,' said the watchman, 'I've just got here.' In the distance two runners approached. The watchman said [and I don't believe this], 'Me thinketh the running of the foremost is like the running of Ahimaaz, the son of Zadok.'

34. When he arrived, it was Cushi, the son of Talal.

He said unto the king, 'All is well, it's your turn to be king.' And he fell down on the earth on his face, it was another nose job. There cometh a second runner, who dresseth like a gorilla. He telleth the king his son Absalom is dead; it was a tasteless Gorillagram. Then Abishai said to David, 'Shall not Shimei [Who?] be put to death because he cursed the Lord's anointed.'

'Wait,' said David, 'are you a Gorillagram without the skin?'

'Nay, lord,' he said.

'No, he shall go free,' said David. 'There'll be no charge at all.' Then he said to Shimei, 'Thou shall not die.'

'Oh, ta,' said Shimei. And Mephibosheth came to see the king. From the day David was dethroned until today Mephibosheth had not washed his feet, shaved his beard, washed his clothes nor had a bath. 'Don't let him near me,' said David.

35. And Mephibosheth bowed low and said, 'I come to serve my lord; what is his wish?'

David said, 'I wish you'd have a bath.' And they useth barge poles and they pusheth Mephibosheth out of the room. Now [here comes another] Barzillai had at one time cooked for David and David said, 'Come thou with me, and I will feed thee with me in Jerusalem.'

And Barzillai said, 'I am this day fourscore years old.'

'Happy birthday to you, happy birthday to you, happy birthday dear Barzillai, happy birthday to you,' sang David.

'What crap,' said Barzillai. 'Can I discern between good and evil? Can thy servant taste what I taste or what I drink? Can I hear any more the voice of singing men and singing women? Wherefore then should thy servant be yet a burden unto my lord the king?'

David smote his forehead, 'For God's sake, someone take this bloody bore away.'

36. And there cometh another little creep, Sheba, son of Bichri. He blew a trumpet, and they said we'll write and let you know. He said, 'We have no part in David PLC: every man to his tents, O Israel [whatever that means].' At that time David took his ten concubines and put them in a ward, he fed them, but went not in unto them, so they were shut up to the day of their death, such was David a Biblical creep. Next, he assembled Joab and Amasa on half pay to go after Sheba, and when they arrived in Gibeon Joab's garment was girded unto him with his sword. As he went forth it fell out and he said to Amasa, 'Art thou in health?' [Why?] Joab took Amasa by the beard to kiss him, and Amasa said, 'Hee! None of that, I'm straight.' Then Joab smote him in the fifth rib and he died. And the Lord blessed him, I think He got it wrong.

37. So Joab and his brother Abishai, both lovely, set off to do a fifth-rib job on Sheba, who was in the city of Thekarzi. So came Joab wearing Chanel No. 5, who trappeth Sheba in Thekarzi. Joab bribeth the people of Thekarzi to kill Sheba promising them timeshare money. They goeth, cut off Sheba's head and tossed it over the wall to Joab, who taketh the catch low down. "Owzat?' he crieth. They throw not the body for on it there beath a donor card for liver and leg transplant.

38. Then Joab, lovely as ever, blew a trumpet; his dentures flew out, and he crieth out: 'Everyone back to his own bed,' and, lo, there cometh cries from many coitus interruptus. When Joab reacheth the frontier, the customs asked, 'What dost thou with this head?'

And he sayeth, 'It is a spare.'

39. There came a famine in the land, and there cometh a hosepipe ban, and David called to the Lord, 'My grass, my grain.'

The Lord speaketh: 'This drought for Saul for slaying the Gibeonites.'

And David said, 'Lord, Saul has been dead this many a day.'

'Yes,' said the Lord, 'I'm running a bit late this year.'

David said to the Gibeonites, 'How can I compensate you? I have Access.'

The Gibeonites said, 'We will have no silver nor gold.' And David giveth a sigh, and maketh them put it in writing.

No, all the Gibeonites wanted was: 'Seven of Saul's sons and we will hang them.'

'Look,' said David, 'make it five and it's a deal.'

40. And in time they hanged them before the Lord and two reporters from *Private Eye*. There came again the Philistines. David and his servants went down, it was silly because the Philistines were up. Among them was the son of giant Ishbibenob and, when David seeth him, his legs goeth, his bottle goeth and finally he goeth. Now in the Philistines was a man with six fingers on each hand, six toes on each foot; he totalleth

twenty-four, and when the battle endeth he hath eleven. The Philistines loseth the war after extra time.

41. Now David commenceth a long, boring grovel to the Lord who is in the flame-resisting burning bush Mark II. 'Oh,' he started, 'the Lord is my rock, and my fortress, and my accountant; Thou savest me from violence. [There went up smoke out of his nostrils and fire out of his mouth with third-degree burns.] He rode upon a cherub, and it collapseth. He made darkness about Him, dark waters and thick clouds of the skies. Visibility was down to ten yards. Before Him coals of fire kindled, cheap, imported Australian brown coal. He drew me out of many waters, mostly heavily polluted. For Thou art my lamp: the Lord will lighten my darkness as will the South-eastern Electricity Board. He maketh my feet like hinds' feet, so I can't wear shoes. He setteth me up in high places, like firemen's ladders. He teacheth my hands to war; so that a bow of steel is broken by mine arms, so I have to buy a new one. The rock of Israel spoke unto me, but they that goeth round listening to rocks should be certified.'

42. But, lo, the Philistines rose again for a return match, and after the battle the Philistine with eleven fingers now had three.

43. Bursting into song, the Lord decided to kindle against the Israelites; why He chose Israel when there was Milton Keynes? The Lord God told David to call a census, and it came to eight hundred thousand people. David's heart smote him, and he taketh an angina tablet. Now came Gad the prophet, who often received

God's mail. He spoke to David for the Lord. 'Three things; thou must choose one. Do you want seven years of famine, or will you flee three months before thine enemies, or do you want three days' pestilence in the land?'

David said, 'They are all bloody awful.'

At this the dear Lord was wrath. He letteth go smoke from his nostrils but it maketh His eyes water. There and then the good Lord sent pestilence upon Israel; David was struck first with haemorrhoids, then there died seventy thousand from the Good Lord's pestilence. And when the angel of the Lord stretched out his hand to destroy Jerusalem, the Lord repented him of the evil (Aww!) and said, 'It is enough.'

'You're bloody right, it's enough,' said the Israelites.

44. Then David started Biblical grovelling. 'Lo, I have sinned, and I have done wickedly, but what have these sheep done?'

'They've crapped all over the meadow that's what,' said the Lord.

'Let Thine hand be against me and my father's house, which is still under offer,' said David, pushing his haemorrhoids back in.

Gad sayeth to David, 'Go, put an altar on Araunah's threshing floor for fifty shekels,' but he put it through the company books as 'Lunch with foreign buyer'. And the plague stopped, but David had to continue with the suppositories.

❧ CHAPTER XIII ❧

NOW KING DAVID WAS VERY OLD, and stricken with years. They covered him with clothes, but he gat [yes, gat] no heat; he was at sixty degrees Fahrenheit, so his physician said, 'Go, find a young virgin and let her lie with the king that he may get heat.' And they found Abishag, and she lay with the king; but, woe, he getteth not heat, it all stayeth hanging down, so they bringeth him hot water bottles that they placeth thereon. While he lieth with it all shrivelled up there cometh a claim on the throne from Adonijah, but David had already made a will leaving the throne and silver fish knives to his son, Solomon.

2. There came Bathsheba, the mother of Solomon, unto David and she said, 'Let my lord king David live for ever.'

And he sayeth, 'I'll do my best.' Hurrying to take over the throne and fish knives cameth Solomon on a souped-up mule (they putteth curry powder under the tail), and the people receiveth him with great joy so that the earth rent with the sound of them; many fell in. Nathan the prophet sayeth, 'Make Solomon the throne and the fish knives are great in the Lord.' And David bowed himself on the bed and getteth stuck there.

God sayeth, 'I will make Solomon's throne greater than yours.' And they started by putting it up on bricks.

3. Now David drew nigh to death and he sayeth to Solomon, 'Be strong, show thyself to be a man, but do not show too much or thou shall be arrested.' Meantime, Adonijah, pretender and creep, asketh Bathsheba to asketh Solomon if he could marry Abishag as he needeth more heat. Bathsheba goeth to ask the king; he caused a seat be set for her − she sat on his right hand, the other one was free.

4. King Solomon sneezed and the throne came off its bricks. He sayeth to Bathsheba, 'Why doth Adonijah wish Abishag for a wife? Knoweth he not she hath no heat? It is too late; I have sentenced Adonijah to death.'

'That could proveth fatal,' said Bathsheba, trying to raise a laugh.

And Adonijah heard the news and he and his ass fled. Solomon set Benaiah after him; and he fell on him and he died. Then Solomon was told that little shit Joab was hiding in the tabernacle. Solomon said to Benaiah, 'Go, fall on him.' And he fell on him and he died. The king put Benaiah in a B&B to await the next assassination.

5. And they brought before Solomon Shimei, and Solomon shook him by the lapels and, lo, they came off. 'Thou knowest all the wickedness thou did to my father David.' The servants of Solomon then hurled Shimei through a plate glass window; hardly had he landed when Solomon called Benaiah: 'Go, fall on him.' So

Benaiah went to fall on him, but missed and Benaiah said unto Solomon, 'Falling on them doesn't kill them so easily, I had to lay on Adonijah for two days before he snuffed it. Can I use a club?' So he goeth forth and he sayeth unto Shimei, 'Would you like to join my club?' then hit him with it.

6. Now Solomon made affinity with Pharaoh king of Egypt. Solomon showed him the riches of Israel, the fish knives and fifty shekels in loose change. He seeth the Pharaoh's daughter and she giveth off a lot of heat. The Lord came parked outside in a pillar of cloud. 'What wouldst thou?'

7. Solomon grovelleth and sayeth, 'O Lord my God [full title], Thou hast made thy servant king instead of David my father.'

'That's because he's dead,' sayeth the Lord.

Solomon sayeth, 'I am but a little child. I know not how to go out or come in.'

'You must be thick,' sayeth the Lord. 'All you do is open the door, go out, turn round and come back in.'

'Oh thank you, Lord,' grovelled the little creep, 'thou givest away state secrets.'

8. There came unto Solomon two women and a child and they both claimeth the child as theirs, and Solomon [my brain hurts] said, 'Give me a sword. I will split the child in two and you can have half each.'

And one woman sayeth, 'No, give the other woman the child.' And Solomon knoweth her to be the mother. He knoweth not how to go out or come in, but he could recognise the real mother. All Israel heard of the judgement and that the wisdom of the Lord was in him. Meanwhile, he practised walking in and out of doors.

9. Now there were princes in the land – Azariah, son of Zadok, Elihoreph and Ahiah, sons of Shisha, Benaiah, son of Jehoiada – they all went on to be clues in *Daily Telegraph* crosswords. Now Israel dwelt safely, every man under his fig tree. If thou travelled there you'd see thousands of men standing under fig trees, if they stood under a banana tree they were disqualified. And God gave Solomon wisdom and largeness of heart; for this latter condition he had a bypass. He spake three thousand proverbs. 'A stitch in time saves nine,' he said. His songs were a thousand and five; none made the charts. All people came to hear his wisdom. 'Let sleeping dogs lie,' he said, and they murmured in awe at his wisdom. 'You can't make a silk purse out of a sow's ear,' he said. Here was wisdom.

10. He gave two shows at the palace each day, a matinee at five and the late show at eight. His agent said, 'You're wowing them, Solly boy.'

He used to start with: 'You can lead a horse to water but you can't make him drink,' and finish with 'A fool and his money are soon parted.' King Hiram of Tyre sent Solomon presents, for Hiram was ever a lover of David, it just didn't get in the papers, that's all.

11. When alone Solomon spoke of trees; he spoke of hyssop that 'springeth out of walls'. He spoketh of beasts and of fowl, and of creeping things, of fishes, of songbirds that goeth tweet tweet.' And his psychiatrist sayeth, 'You're not getting better, Solly.'

12. Now Solomon wished to build a temple for the Lord and getteth Hiram to send him cedar trees, and starteth the destruction of the cedars of Lebanon. In exchange, Solomon giveth Hiram many measures of wheat, twenty measures of pure oil and fifty packets of crisps. When the temple was finished it was dedicated by the priests, but the Lord filled the house with cloud, and they all stumbled and crasheth into each other. And Solomon gropeth his way to the altar, and blessed the congregation, and the Bradford & Bingley. But when the cloud cleared there was no one there. And Solomon spread forth his hands towards heaven, but they wouldn't reach. To further ingratiate himself with the Lord, he offered up two and twenty thousand oxen and a hundred and twenty thousand sheep – after that there was bugger-all left. For seven days they feasted and they goeth home fulfilled and a stone heavier. The Sabbath day Solomon knelt before the altar with his hands raised towards the sky. When he goeth to rise his knees seizeth up and they taketh him away in a wheelbarrow.

13. To the accompaniment of the Lord playing the bellows on a bagpipe, Solomon said, 'If there be famine, if there be pestilence, mildew, locust, or if there be caterpillar, or plague; if the enemy besiege thee, the most harmless plague of these is the caterpillar.' And they all gave thanks unto the Lord.

The Lord now spake from a volcano with scorched legs. 'Hear, O Israel, thou shall know every man the plague in his own heart.' [Heart plague, a rare Biblical disease caused by standing under fig trees.] And it came to pass that Hiram sent Solomon sixscore talents of gold, and straightaway Solomon put them in the futures market.

14. Now Pharaoh king of Egypt had attacked Gezer, set it on fire and slain the people. He then gave it as a present to his daughter, who was Solomon's wife. She sayeth unto her father, 'Thank you for giving me a burning city full of dead people.'

15. When the queen of Sheba heard of the fame of Solomon walking in and out of doors, she journeyed to see him to prove him with hard questions like, 'Why doth the chicken cross the road?'

And he sayeth, 'A fool and his money are soon parted.'

And she looketh at him in wonder and sayeth, 'I knew not that's what maketh a chicken cross the road.'

Then he really turned on: 'Old soldiers never die, they only fade away,' he said. He clapped his hands and a servant came forth and showed her the fish knives, and she saw the mark of the Lord on them, EPNS. And she returneth home full of wisdom with Solomon's last words ringing in her ears, 'You can't dresseth mutton as lamb.'

16. A little environmental snippet. And the king made of the almug tree pillars for the house of the Lord. There came no more almug trees, nor have any been seen unto this day. The erosion of the planet had started – with Solomon the Wise. King Solomon loved many strange women: the daughter of Pharaoh, women of the Moabites, Ammonites, Hittites and Battersea. At the last count, he had seven hundred wives and three

hundred concubines. It was nearly worn away and he taketh steroids, and he taketh down the ceiling mirrors.

17. Solomon the Wise wanted something different, so he worshippeth Ashtoreth, the kinky goddess of leather accessories. Then he got in deep. He built an altar to Chemosh [Who?], the abomination of Moab. He made burnt offerings to it – steak, chips, beans on toast. There was no end to the degradation and the *Jewish Chronicle* wrote, 'Solomon and wives go kinky in Chemosh ritual, police arrest thirteen.' The Lord was wrath and His pillar of cloud goeth all squiggley and He calleth out, 'Solomon, Solomon, what has thou done?'

And Solomon sayeth, 'Well, now that you've asked me, I've done seven hundred wives, three hundred concubines and Doris.'

The Lord sayeth, 'Has thou told the Guinness Book of Records?'

18. And the Lord stirred up an adversary unto Solomon, Hadad the Edomite. After this brief mention Hadad the Edomite disappears from the Bible.

19. Apart from bronchitis the only threat to Solomon was Jeroboam, who went on to become a measure of champagne. He was coming out of Jerusalem, and there came a loony prophet, Ahijah, who found himself in the way. He was clad in a new garment and Ahijah caught the new garment and rent it in twelve pieces; you could see everything. The loony then said, 'Take thee ten pieces: thus sayeth the Lord of Israel. Behold, I will rend the kingdom out of the hand of Solomon, ha-ha-ha-ho-ho-ho-he-he-he.'

Jeroboam watched as the attendants put on his strait-jacket. Solomon sought to kill Jeroboam with an attack of death, and Jeroboam fleeth like the clappers to Egypt, and he hath a laundry problem.

20. About now king Solomon died; on his death certificate, cause of death, wives. At the funeral the wives threw themselves on the grave and it caveth in and they hath to start all over again. To decide who was to be king they had a raffle. It was won by Rehoboam and he getteth the throne and the fish knives. He said to the people, 'My father made your yoke heavy; he also chastised you with whips.'

'He was kinky,' said a voice.

'I', said Rehoboam, 'will chastise you with scorpions.'

'He's kinky too,' said a voice, and the people goeth to their tents in gloom.

To cheer them up Rehoboam sent a joker to soothe them and he sayeth, 'Hello folks, you know what a Jewish dilemma is? Pork chops at half price.' And all Israel stoned him with stones and he died.

21. Now while Rehoboam ruled over Judah, Jeroboam, on a show of hands and money, became king of Israel, with a company pension included. Jeroboam built a house on Mount Ephraim but it was timeshare and after three weeks he had to move out. Whereupon the king took counsel and made two calves of gold and [wait for it] he said unto them: 'It is too much for you to go up to Jerusalem: behold thy gods.'

22. And that's what he was doing when they came to take him away. He sendeth one calf to Bethel and one

to Dan; this was a sin, and from a cloud there cometh rumbling from the Lord and He was wrath for, around the golden calves, they whoopeth it up and get pissed. Many old soldiers doeth the last turkey in the shops. A man of God came by, singing king Solomon's greatest hits. Jeroboam said, 'Great, convert thy house and do a cabaret and I will reward thee in cash.'

And the man of God said, 'The Lord sayeth I will not go with thee, neither will I eat bread nor drink water.'

But an old prophet of Bethel talketh him into it and he came and drank Highland Spring water and ate wholemeal bread with Marmite. The Lord was wrath with rage. He set the man on an ass, on the way a lion set on him and it slayeth him. So endeth a man of God.

23. And the Lord spoke from a fiery bush, the temperature inside being 102 degrees Fahrenheit. He poureth with sweat and He loseth a stone. He called out, 'I will bring evil on the house of Jeroboam; I shalt increase the mortgage payments and I will cut off from Jeroboam that which pisseth against the wall, I will take away the remnants of his house, as a man taketh away dung, till it be all gone.' Despite this warning, when Jeroboam stepped outside he treadeth in it. When Jeroboam was nine hundred he died. They buried him standing up for it was cheaper. Now his nit of a son with a name like floor cleaner, Nadab, ruled.

24. And Rehoboam, the son of Solomon, reigned in Judah. He died of the deafness; there cometh a steamroller behind him and he heareth it not. His son with a name like a conserve, Abijam, ascended the throne, but

tripped, fell, broke his neck and died. As he was only five foot three his was the shortest reign on record. His son with a name liketh the logo for an engineering company, Asa, mounted the throne, but had to wait 'till they'd got his father's body off. Asa did that which was right in the eyes of the Lord. He starteth at the bottom, he took away the sodomites and closed all gay bars. He removed all the idols his father had made. He also removed his mother Maachah from being queen because she had made an idol in a grove, Gary Glitter. Then bad news for Asa, he dieth and the obituary in the *Jewish Chronicle* sayeth: 'King Asa dead, fish knives for sale.'

25. And they goeth to his son Jehoshaphat and said, 'Good news, your father's dead, you're king.' Meanwhile, Nadab reigned in Israel and he did evil in the sight of the Lord. He swingeth cats around by the tail, he throweth banana skins in front of old ladies and he putteth Clingfilm over toilets. But Baasha conspired against him and Baasha smote him at Gibbethon; it was only a glancing smote, leaving a bruised knee. Baasha was heartbroken that he hadn't killed him so he went and killed Asa and reigned in his stead.

26. And when he reigned he smote all the houses of Jeroboam, he smote all the windows and naileth up the toilet doors, and putteth Superglue in the locks. Now the Lord dredgeth up another ninny to keep the Bible going: Jehu, son of Hanani, who was a haddock stretcher at a fish-squirting factory. And the Lord said to the creep, 'Jehu, I have exalted thee out of the dust [He found him in a garbage can], and made thee prince

over Israel, and thou [He's going to change his mind again] hast made my people of Israel to sin.'

'How could I?' sayeth Jehu, 'I've only just come out of a dustbin.'

'Silence when you speak to me,' sayeth the Lord. 'He that dieth of Baasha [Dr, Dr, I think I've got Baasha] shall the dogs eat; woe to them that give them Pal.' Then came the word of the Lord against Baasha, the word was 'overdraft'. Baasha rent his clothes, beat his breast causing multiple bruising, he then dieth.

27. There be Zimri, captain of chariots. One night he getteth drunk on Château Latour 1900 BC, a deep, smooth, velvety taste balanced with very little acid, good with red meat. He staggereth to Asa and smote him dead, and Zimri became king. His first kingly duty was to slay all the house of Baasha; it was terrible, they had to disinfect the place. Wonderful – from piss artist to king in one go!

28. A resumé: according to the Lord, all the people of Judah and Israel are each and every one committing evil, the frustrating part is, apart from sodomy, no one knows what these evils are. After Zimri, the piss artist, had destroyed the house of Baasha, it says, 'He left him not one that pisseth against a wall.' There goeth around that Zimri hath killed Asa; the autopsy sayeth it was his fifth rib, and they appointed Omri, Asa's accountant, to sue Zimri for damages leading to a severe case of death, but Zimri sayeth he is bankrupt. Omri gathereth an army and attacked Zimri, but his bottle goeth, and he burnt the king's house and his bank statements over

him with fire and he died. He was cooked to a nicety, like one of Bernard Matthews' turkeys he was 'bootiful'.

29. The people of Israel were divided in two parts: half followed Tibni, the other half Omri – they settled their differences very easily, Omri killed Tibni. And, here it comes again, Omri wrought evil in the eyes of the Lord, and did worse than all before him. He wore his underpants back to front, feeleth little girls' bicycle saddles, and he showeth himself like one of the Chippendales. It came to pass, Omri slept with his fathers and was buried; a nasty thing to do to a person when he's only asleep.

30. Ahab, his son, now ruled; he hath all the charisma of an out-of-order phone box. And Ahab did evil in sight of the Lord (His pillar of cloud overlooked Ahab), he eateth hamsters.

31. And from B&Q he buildeth a do-it-yourself altar to Baal. The Lord striketh the land with drought, and, lo, there was a ban on chariot washing. And the prophet Elijah, who was on income support, said unto Ahab, 'No rain shall fall these years.'

And the Lord spoke from in a thundercloud and He goeth deaf, 'Get thee hence,' so Elijah got hence. 'Turn thee east and go to Cherith.'

'But, Lord,' said Elijah, 'Cherith is west.'

'Is it?' said the Lord, 'go west then; I have commanded ravens to feed thee.'

Elijah got to Cherith and the ravens brought him bread and flesh to eat, but Elijah complaineth and they bringeth him instead a Cornish pasty, peas and chips.

Then he asketh the Lord for apple pie and custard and, lo, the ravens bringeth it, and a bill for thirty shekels. And Elijah crieth out, 'Lord, I am skint,' and the Lord blessed him. 'That's no bloody good,' said Elijah.

32. 'Arise,' said the Lord.

'I'm up as high as I can get,' said Elijah.

'Go,' said the Lord, 'to Zarephath; there a woman will sustain thee.'

So Elijah, the prophet, sponger and scrounger, went thence – and saw the woman and started to scrounge. 'Woman, bring me, I pray, a morsel of bread.'

She sayeth, 'I have none, but I have a handful of meal in a barrel, and a little oil in a cruse.'

'That'll do,' said the hungry bugger. And he lived on the woman many days until her food runneth out, and Elijah doeth a moonlight.

33. The Lord said unto Elijah, 'Go into the desert and show thyself unto Ahab and I will send rain.' So Elijah and Ahab meeteth face to face; a nasty shock for both of them. The Lord sent rain and they were both soaked. As an encore the Lord sent a famine.

34. And Elijah challenged Ahab as to who was the true god, the Lord or Baal. 'Kill two bullocks, one for you, one for me – place them on wood – you call Baal to set fire and I will call on the Lord.' Ahab calleth for fire, it cometh not; then Elijah called the Lord and, lo, the fire lighted. And Elijah said, 'Well, there goes your god, Baal.'

But some still believeth and say, 'Please, can we have our Baal back.'

Ahab taketh down the altar to Baal. 'I'll never go to B&Q again,' he said. And Elijah repaired the altar of the true Lord, using plaster board and Araldite. To wind up the end of Baal, Elijah sayeth, 'Take the false prophets of Baal down to the river.' There Elijah slew them. Good old Elijah. The *Jewish Chronicle* said 'God beats Baal in setting fire to oxen.'

35. Elijah said unto Ahab, 'Celebrate, go eat and drink,' and he did, while Elijah went to the top of Mount Carmel with sandwiches, and he cast himself on the earth and spraineth both wrists. He put his head between his knees and, lo, he can seeth up his bum. The hand of the Lord was on Elijah; and he girded up his loins, which took some time as he was well endowed in that area. Elijah went into the wilderness, Slough.

36. He called to the Lord, 'Take away my life for I am not better than my father's.' People who had seen his say it was much better than his fathers. Rather than pay for a room, Elijah goeth in a cave and the Lord sayeth unto him, 'What doest thou here, Elijah?'

'I draweth a circle in the sand, then I stand in it on one leg and I whistle "My Yiddisher Mama", then I leap out of the circle and I shout "Stop that whistling",' said Elijah.

The Lord sendeth down an angel with Valium tablets. The Lord said to Elijah, 'Go and stand on a mountain before the Lord.' Behold, the Lord passed by a strong wind, rent the mountain and Elijah bloweth over. After the wind cometh the earthquake; it splitteth the ground and Elijah fell in.

Then comest a great fire storm and Elijah calleth, 'Lord, Lord, come down.'

The Lord sayeth, 'No, it's too dangerous.'

37. It came to pass that Ahab spoke to Naboth saying, 'Give me thy vineyard, and I will give ye a better vineyard of Cabernet Sauvignon.'

And Naboth sayeth, 'No, I prefer my Traminer grapes.'

Ahab goeth white with anger and red with anger, turning him into a delightful pink colour. He goeth to his bedroom, laid him down on his bed, and turned away his face, cricking his neck.

Jezebel, his wife, heard the crack; she asketh him what ailed him, he telleth her about Naboth. 'The little shit,' she said, 'leave him to me.' So Ahab left him to her. She taketh football yobboes and they stoned Naboth to death. He never recovered from the shock. Jezebel telleth Ahab, 'I've killed Naboth for you.'

He sayeth, 'You little darling.'

38. And the Lord speaketh, with a wobbly voice from inside a jelly, 'In the place where dogs licked the blood of Naboth, shall they lick thy blood, rhesus negative. I will bring evil on thee like haemorrhoids and will cut off from Ahab him that pisseth against the wall.'

'Lord,' sayeth Ahab, 'please don't cut mine off, I'm the only one that pisseth against the wall; the loo is out of order.'

The Lord said, 'I will make thine house like the house of Jeroboam.'

'That will need two extra bedrooms, another toilet, a patio with plastic windbreaks,' sayeth Ahab.

And the Lord sayeth, 'The dogs shall eat Jezebel by the wall of Jezreel.'

'Oh,' said Ahab, 'can't they have her from a bowl?'

But Ahab was feared of the Lord's threat of haemorrhoids and a sore arse, so he rent his clothes, he putteth on rancid sackcloth, he putteth ash on his face and dirt on his head. And Jezebel sayeth, 'You scruffy bugger, you're not coming into the palace like that, I've only just had the throne cleaned and dusted.'

39. It came to pass that the Israelites went to war with the Syrians and Ahab asked the prophet Micaiah which way the battle would go and he speaketh gobbledegook. 'When thou shalt go into an inner chamber and hide thyself.'

Then sayeth the king, 'Put this fellow in prison, feed him bread of affliction and with wafer of affliction.'

40. But the jailer sayeth, 'We only haveth wholemeal and Perrier.' And Ahab goeth to war and a certain man [observers say they were pretty certain it was a man] drew a bow and smote the king of Israel between the joints of the harness.

And Ahab crieth out, 'Driver, turn the meter off, stop the chariot.' And he dieth without paying the driver, and he bleedeth all over the chariot and the driver receiveth compensation through the small claims court. They carrieth Ahab's body back in state and the physician sayeth, 'In his condition the best thing is to bury him.'

41. Now his son, Ahaziah, reigned in his stead. And a spotty herbert, the son of Asa, called Jehoshaphat, a name that sounded like a fat bum being smacked, ascended the

throne of Judah. He walked in the ways of his father into doors, walls and lamp posts. And he did that which was not right in the sight of the Lord. He picketh his nose and flicked them at the cat, and he walked in the way of his father and in the way of his mother, which was the other direction, and he knoweth not whether he cometh or goeth. And the sodomites he removeth from the land, so that people could bend down with safety. And Jehoshaphat slept with his fathers, and was buried with them.

❦ CHAPTER XIV ❦

ABOUT NOW AHAZIAH, SON OF AHAB, fell down through a lattice in his upper chamber; why would one put lattice over a chamber? The Lord works in mysterious ways, this was another one of them.

2. And the king asked what manner of man was Elijah and they said, 'He was an hairy man, girt with a girdle of leather about his loins.'

'Oh kinky, eh?' sayeth the king. To make himself look taller Elijah sat on a mountain. The king sent fifty men. They sayeth to him, 'The king sayeth, come down.'

3. 'I'm buggered if I will,' sayeth Elijah. 'Tell you what, if I be a man of God, then let fire come down and consume thee.'

A smoke alarm goeth too late, fire cometh down from heaven and consumed all fifty and the Lord sayeth, 'Did I get them?'

'Spot on,' sayeth Elijah and resetteth the smoke alarm.

Again the king sent fifty men and they said, 'Elijah, the king says come down quickly.'

He sayeth, 'If I be a man of God, etc., let fire, etc., come down and consume thee, etc.' The smoke alarm goeth and fire cometh down, etc., and consumed them all. And Elijah sweepeth up the ashes and put them on the tomato plants. There came again fifty men but this time they weareth asbestos suits. Behold, the angel of the Lord cometh and said, 'The Lord is out of firelighters – pray go down to the king.' So Elijah goeth and speaketh to the king, 'Thus saith the Lord. Thou shalt not come down off that bed on which thou art gone up, thou shall die.' So the king died.

4. The Lord had promised Elijah he would take him to heaven by a whirlwind. Elijah said could he take his friend Elisha [new prophet], but the Lord sayeth it was only a single-seater whirlwind. And people said to Elisha, 'Knowest thou the Lord will take away thy master from thy head today?'

'I didn't know my master was on my head,' said Elisha.

5. Elijah sayeth unto Elisha, 'Tarry here.' So Elisha had a good tarry lasting thirty minutes; the world's record for a tarry is thirty-eight. Then they departed for the River Jordan; there Elijah took his mantle and smote the waters, and they divided hither and thither.

'Look what you've done, Elijah,' said Elisha, 'you've hithered and thithered the waters.' Then he speaketh mumbo jumbo. 'Before they take you away from me, let a double measure of thy spirit be mine.'

'I've only got bells,' said Elijah.

'Yes, I know,' said Elisha, 'I can hear them.'

And then, behold, the Lord sent down a chariot of fire, and horses of fire, and Elijah was taketh to heaven, all the while calling for the fire brigade and trying to beat the flames out. Then Elisha took up Elijah's mantle that he'd dropped in panic, and he went back and stood by the bank of the Jordan, but they didn't open until ten o'clock and Elisha called, 'Where is the Lord God of Elijah?'

And a voice from heaven calleth, 'He's up here, trying to put the fire out.'

Then Elisha took hold of his clothes and rent them in two, his underpants giveth away and, lo, he was exposed even unto his members, which were at their best in the sunlight.

6. He went thence to Bethel to have a wig fitted. There came forth little children who shouteth, 'Go up, thou bald head; baldy, where's yer wig?'

And he cursed them. 'You little bastards, bugger off.'

But they bugger not off, then came from out of the wood two she bears and they killed and ate forty and two children. Then Elisha, the man of God, went to Mount Carmel to test his new wig for wind resistance.

7. Now Jehoram, the son of Ahab, began to reign over Israel, and he wrought evil in the sight of the Lord. At parties he would let go a butler's revenge*. And Mesha, king of Moab, rendered unto the king of Israel a hundred thousand lambs and a hundred thousand rams, so for months after they were all treading in sheep shit. And the king of Israel complaineth about all the shit, and the king of Moab was wrath and so started

---

* A lethal, quiet fart

the Biblical sheepshit wars. So Israel, Judah and Edom all joined forces to attack Moab as they were all fearful of any more sheepshit. King Jehoshaphat said, 'Which way shall we attack?'

And Jehoram sayeth, 'Through the wilderness of Edom.'

'Isn't that the B2039?' said Jehoshaphat.

'Yes,' said Jehoram, 'we join it at the intersection of the B319.' Before battle they bringeth a minstrel to give the troops heart and he singeth 'My Yiddisher Mama', and the hand of the Lord came upon him, making it very difficult to play.

8. Then the Lord giveth the battle briefing: 'Ye shall smite every city, fell all good trees, stop all wells and water, mar every piece of good land with stones.' It was an environmental disaster. Then the Israelites rose up and smote the Moabites, and they retreateth, but the Israelites went forward and smote them, they even went sideways and smote them. It taketh three smotes to kill a Moabite, but some were doing five and six — a complete waste of smotes. Now the king of Moab saw that he was being outsmoted, so he taketh his son and offered him for a burnt offering upon the wall. There was great indignation against Israel, the king of Moab taketh off his son, instead for a burnt offering he roasteth a Safeways' chicken.

9. There crieth a woman, 'Boo hoo.'

And Elisha sayeth, 'What ails thee?'

She sayeth, 'Lo! The creditors came to take my furniture away.'

Elisha sayeth, 'What have you got in the house?'

And she sayeth, 'Nothing, save a pot of oil.'

Elisha bringeth several empty pots; he waveth his arms over them and sayeth, 'Abracadabra.' And, yes, all the pots were full of oil, which she selleth for two hundred shekels, and all was well.

10. One day Elisha passed through Shunem where a great woman constrained him to eat bread. It tasted so good that Elisha continually passed by for the hand-out.

The great woman said to her husband, 'That man is a holy man of God.'

'No, he isn't,' said her husband, 'he's a bloody scrounger.'

The wife said, 'Let us make a little chamber on the wall, and let us set in there a bed, a stool and a candlestick.'

'He's not bloody moving in is he?' said the husband, filling in divorce papers.

Sure enough, Elisha came thither; he climbed into the chamber and lay there scratching his parts, his rent problems solved. He sayeth to Gehazi, his servant [he's skint and he's got a servant], 'Call the woman.' The woman cometh, and Elisha sayeth, 'Have you got any more of that bread?'

She answered, 'I dwell among my people' [Eh?].

'Of course, you do,' said Elisha. 'Is there anything I can do for you?'

And Gehazi said, 'She hath no child.'

'Can I be of help?' sayeth Elisha, taking off his clothes. Then she let go with a Biblical bafflement. 'Nay, my lord, thou man of God do not lie unto thy hand-maiden.'

Bits of smouldering cloth falleth from heaven. 'That must be Elijah,' said Elisha, 'he's trying to get in touch.'

11. She beareth a son and he grew up, which is the right direction. She calleth him Eyeshigher, because one eye was higher, but overwhelmed by his mother's chicken soup, he collapsed. They took him to his mother, she sat him on her knees 'till noon, then he died. At the autopsy they sayeth he dieth from being kept on his mother's knees too long. And the mother ran to Elisha; she caught him by the feet, he goeth arse over tip. She taketh the prophet to her son, and he waveth a wand over him and sayeth, 'Abracadabra, upsydaisy.' The child doth not upsydaisy – then the loony prophet stretched himself over the lad and the child sneezed seven times and opened his eyes. 'You've got a cold coming,' sayeth Elisha.

The child arose and said to Elisha, 'Ta.'

The mother sobbeth, she throweth herself at Elisha's feet and arse over tip he goeth again.

12. And Elisha came to Gilgal. There was a dearth on the land; the sons of the prophets were sitting in the dearth. Elisha said unto his servant, 'Set on the great pot, and seethe pottage for the sons of the prophet currently in the dearth.' So they poured out for the men to eat in the dearth. They were eating the pottage when they cried out, 'Man of God, there is death in the pot.'

Elisha was puzzled, he didn't remember putting death

in the pottage, so he changeth it all for beans and, lo, there came many seat-lifters.

13. Now there was Naaman, a great man, captain of the Syrian Army. He goeth to a physician and sayeth, 'I think I have leprosy.'

The physician asketh, 'How do you know?'

And Naaman sayeth, 'My fingers keep falling off.' Then Naaman heard of Elisha and his miracles and he maketh an appointment. When they meeteth, Elisha sayeth, 'Does thou want this on NHS or privately?'

'I'm with Private Patients Plan,' sayeth Naaman.

Then Elisha writeth out a prescription. 'Immerse thyself seven times in the Jordan; that and a bottle of antibiotics.'

Lo, the treatment worked. Naaman sayeth, 'Thou hast cured me, how can I thank you, what would you like?'

'Money,' sayeth Elisha.

14. The sons of the prophets said unto Elisha, 'The place where we dwell is too straight for us.'

'Right,' sayeth Elisha, 'but I'm straight as well.'

They goeth to Jordan to build an unstraight house, they cutteth down trees. Now comes a delightful story. As one was felling a tree, the axehead fell in the river, and he crieth out, 'Master, master, it's fallen in the water.'

'Where fell it?' said Elisha. He shewed him the place. Elisha took a stick and cast it thither; and the iron did swim. Elisha said, 'Take it up to thee.' And he put out his hand and took it; and so ends another tale.

15. For the umpteenth time the king of Syria warred against Israel. He took counsel with his servants, saying, 'In such and such a place shall be my camp.'

But Elisha, the little sneak, runneth to the king of Israel, and sayeth, 'Beware, thou go not to such and such a place, the Syrians are there.'

The Syrian secret service put the finger on Elisha. They told the king, 'Elisha telleth the king of Israel even words thou speaketh in thy bedchamber like, "Darling, where's the po?"'

16. The king of Syria waxed wrath, and it dripped all over him. 'Go, fetch me that creep Elisha and I'll cut his balls off.'

So a hit squad goeth to cut his balls off; they surroundeth his home. Elisha seeth them with garden shears and he putteth on an armoured jockstrap. And he calleth out, 'Lord, save my balls,' and the good Lord smiteth the hit squad with blindness. And Elisha sayeth, 'Follow me.' They seeth not, but in the Bible all is possible. So the blind men followed Elisha; when they arrived at such and such a place the Lord opened their eyes and, lo, they were surrounded by the king of Israel. [How he did it on his own is another Biblical mystery.] 'Shall I smite them?'

'No,' said Elisha, and he calleth to the hit squad. 'Promise thou will not chop off my balls.' And they promised and threw away their garden shears.

17. But the king of Syria waxed wrath again, and he attacked the Israelites; he besieged Samaria, and there was a great famine. An ass's head was sold for fourscore

pieces of silver, and part of a cab of doves' dung for five pieces of silver; what a meal! Boiled ass's head with dung à la pigeon.

18. The king of Israel was hiding from the fighting. There cried a woman, 'Helppp!'

The king said, 'What aileth thee?'

She said, 'This woman said unto me, "Give thy son that we may eat him today, and eat mine tomorrow." So we boiled my son with new potatoes and lentils and we ate him with a full-bodied red. Next day I said, "Give thy son that we may eat him" – but she hath hid her son, and tried to put us off with a tin of beans.'

19. Then the king speaketh more Biblical mumbo jumbo. 'God do so and more also to me, if the head of Elisha, the son of Shaphat, shall stand on him this day.'

And God said, 'I don't know what you're talking about.'

And the king said, 'I'm talking about ten words a minute.' And then the king appointed the lord on whose hand he leaned to have the charge of the gate and [wait for it] the people trode upon him in the gate and he died; another baffling Biblical death!

20. Now the king of Syria was ill and sendeth Hazael, a servant, to Elisha.

The servant sayeth, 'The king is ill, will he live?'

Elisha sayeth, 'What has he got?'

The servant sayeth, 'Flu.'

'Oh yes,' said Elisha, 'he'll live; you don't die from flu.'

Next day the king of Syria dieth of flu and they sendeth out bouncers with iron bars to look for Elisha.

21. In the fifth year of Joram, Jehoram began to reign, and he walked in the way of the kings of Israel; that's why he kept getting run over.

22. Now the loony prophet Elisha called one of the children of the prophets. He said, 'Gird up your loins, take this box of oil, pour it over his head, say "I anoint thee king of Israel" then open the door and run like fuck.' And the boy doeth it all and runneth like fuck.

And Jehu sayeth, 'I've just had an Oilogram.'

And his friends seeth him, saying, 'Wherefore cometh this mad fellow to thee?'

23. 'Well,' he sayeth, 'I am the king of Israel, then he runneth like hell.' Then, unexplainably, all the servants rushed upstairs, each taking his garment with him and putting it under him on the top of the stairs. And they blew loud blasts on the trumpets, giving half of them prolapses. Jehu waxed up his wrath 'till it dripped all over the floor, all his smiting licences were up so he went to smite Joram, who was concubining. Jehu drew nigh to Joram; he could hear the grunting. It was night and from the watchtower the night watchman gobbeth over the battlements, and a cry came from below, 'You dirty bugger.' It was Jehu, who was covered in it.

Then Jehu came unto Joram and said, 'Is there to be peace between us?'

Joram arose from his concubine and sayeth, 'There

can be no peace as the whoredoms of Jezebel and her girls continue.'

'But', said Jehu, who was an investor, 'she's doing well, profits are up eighty per cent, and the FT Index shares have gone up three shekels.'

24. Then Jehu said to Jehoram, a total stranger, 'Stand still and smile.' So he standeth still and smiled, and Jehu shot him. They buried him with one trouser leg rolled up as he was a mason.

25. Then Jehu's appointments' secretary said: 'Sire, it's time for your next smote.' And he goeth to the Rye Golf Club, he taketh king Ahaziah on to the first green and he smote him in one. Jehu was feeling great, did a few kingly press-ups and was ready for some new smiting. And when Jehu came to Jezreel, Jezebel heard of it; she painted her face, tied up her hair and looked out of the window, and when he saw her, he screamed, 'Barbara Cartland!'

26. And there looked out three eunuchs, and Jehu said to them, 'Throw her down.' And they threw her. Some of her blood was sprinkled on the wall and on the horses. 'Don't worry,' said Jehu, 'that will come off with Flash.' Then he trode her underfoot. And the doggies came and eateth her, and Jehu said, 'After this they'll never eat Pedigree Chum.'

27. Now blood and more blood. Ahab had seventy sons, all with different tutors. And Jehu wrote asking them to return. But no, they were ambushed by Jehu who cut off their heads [the slaughter goes on, folks] and put them in baskets and sent them to Jezreel. Jehu

said, 'Lay ye the heads neatly in two heaps at the entering in of the city gate.' But the police said it would cause hold-ups and fainting. Jehu went on to slay all the house of Ahab, except the parrot. 'Cat And Parrot Survive Slaughter,' said the *Jewish Chronicle*.

28. Jehu meeteth Jehonadab and said, 'Is thine heart right, as my heart is right?'

'No,' said Jehonadab, 'I've got a heart murmur. Give me thine hand.' He did so and Jehonadab gave Jehu his knee. Then Jehu went to Samaria. He called all those who worship Baal to worship, then he smote them all. He broke the house of Baal and made it a draught house, and until today it only sells beer and snacks. And the Lord said to Jehu, 'Bless thou, thou hast done well in executing that which is right in mine eyes.'

29. When Athaliah saw that her son Ahaziah was dead, she selleth all his clothes to the Red Cross. And Jehoiada, a priest, calleth all the great captains to shew them the king's son [whoever he is] and he announceth to the crowd, 'This is the king's son.' The people rejoiced; they blew trumpets and got ruptures. But from a window Athaliah came to the people in the temple and the Lord, rent her clothes and she sheweth two beauties. She crieth out, 'Treason, treason.'

'Never mind treason,' they said, 'look at those boobs.'

Jehoiada calleth the woman; he giveth them a quick squeeze, then said, 'Take her hence.' And in good old Biblical style they took her forth and slew her. All of the people of the city rejoiced, then whooped! They slew

Athaliah, it was a lovely end to the day, and a crowd of bloodthirsty Biblical bastards.

30. Now Elisha, the loony prophet, had fallen sick of the sickness; soon he would be dead of the deadness. Joash, king of Israel, came and wept over him; Elisha got soaked, and died of pneumonia. His last words were, 'Someone call a doctor.' After he was dead, they buried him up a tree; he had always wanted people to look up to him. And many people sought a miracle by touching the body of Elisha, and they carried a dead man up the tree who touched the bones of Elisha, click, click, and, lo, the dead man recovereth. 'I have never felt better,' he said. Then he falleth from the tree and died.

31. Now the next dozy character is king Amaziah. He did all things as Joash, his father, had done except die. The high places were not taken away, so those people in penthouses were safe from rent increases. As yet people did sacrifices and burnt incense on the high places so the landlords banned all rooftop barbecues. And it came to pass, as soon as the kingdom was confirmed, king Amaziah slew his servants. This made a big difference in household bills. Jehoash sent Amaziah a message saying, 'The thistle that was in Lebanon sent to the cedar that was in Lebanon.'

Amaziah sent it back saying, 'Sorry, it's all double dutch – is it supposed to be funny? Come, let us meet face to face.' So they went up and met face to face, and it was a nasty shock for both of them, 'No, Lord, no.'

32. Jeroboam, son of Jehoash, restored the coast of

Israel from the entering of Hamath unto the sea of the plains, the only mention in the Old Testament of an effort to save the environment, then he died. Before he did he asked to see the fish knives.

33. With the death of Amaziah of Judah his son Azariah, aged sixteen started to rule. He was a spotty lad with big ears that kept him permanently in the shade. He did that which was right in the sight of the Lord; he grovelled before him. But there were those who sinned against the Lord, so the Lord smote the innocent, spotty Azariah with leprosy 'till the day of his death. By the time he died there wasn't much of him left. Then Jotham, his son, ruled Judah.

34. First Shallum smote Zachariah, then Menahem smote Shallum, then Tiphsah, then he smote all the women with child then a captain of the guard smote Pekahiah, then Hoshea smote Pekah (twice in one day). The *Jewish Chronicle* said, 'Outbreak Of Smoting In Holy Land.'

35A. Now Hoshea ruled in Samaria, a sort of Jewish Peckham Rye, but Zonka king of Assyria waxed wrath at Hoshea for he sendeth not his monthly tithe of smoked salmon, Bovril and Paxo stuffing. So he put Hoshea in prison, and he sayeth, 'How long will I be in here?'

And the king sayeth, 'Not long, it's timeshare.' Now the Lord was wrath with the Israelites as the men eateth lobster and bacon sandwiches, and the women weareth not knickers, and they built high places at exorbitant rents and they wrote sinful graffiti, 'Bum to God'. And in the high places they burn incense and smoke themselves out. And the Lord speaketh from a thick sea mist and He collideth with a ship. 'Turn ye from your evil ways,' He sayeth.

And they sayeth, 'Piss off.' So using a funnel He did. Now Hoshea did right in the sight of the Lord. He removed the high places, broke the images, cut down the groves, broke in pieces the brazen serpent of Moses; the damages ran into thousands of shekels.

35B. And the Lord was with him and Hoshea prospered; the gown shop and the delicatessen were doing well. He rebelled against the king of Syria and sendeth not smoked salmon, Bovril nor Paxo. For this the king of Syria attacked Samaria and captured it; he taketh away all smoked salmon, Bovril and Paxo.

36A. Now Hezekiah, king of Judah, was afraid of the Assyrian king and as a peace offering he sent Sennacherib peace offerings. He cut off the gold from the doors of the temple, he took the pillars away and the roof falleth in. It came to pass, Hezekiah rent his clothes, covered himself with sackcloth and crap. He said, 'O Lord God, who dwellest between the cherubims, who speaketh with difficulty from fiery bushes, clouds, thick sea mists and jellies, the king of Assyria hath destroyed the nation, all the smoked salmon, Bovril and Paxo have gone and all I have left is the Oil of Ulay and the hereditary fish knives. Three years have the Assyrians stayed, during which I have digged and drunk strange waters, Highland Spring, Badoit, Malvern, and Perrier, and with the sole of my feet I have dried up all the rivers of besieged places.'

The Lord said, 'My son, I knew not you could drink water through your feet.'

It came to pass, an angel of the Lord gave the Assyrian camp a terrible smoting: and when they arose early in the morning, behold, they were all dead corpses; not one corpse was left alive, and Hezekiah gave thanks to the Good Lord.

36B. In those days was Hezekiah sick unto death. He had been drinking water through his foot and fell ill. Then came cheerful Charlie, Isaiah, he said: 'Set thy house in order for thou shalt die.' Then the Lord spoke from a waterfall, all the while being washed downstream: 'Listen not to Isaiah; he is a miserable sod, you will not die.'

'Oh, thanks, God,' said Hezekiah.

But the Lord heareth not, being washed out to sea.

Then Isaiah prophesieth, 'Come the day when your sons will be taken by Babylonians as eunuchs.'

'My boys', sayeth Hezekiah, 'have their balls chopped, oh no.'

37. Now it came to pass, Josiah came to the throne. He doeth what is right, he walked in the way of David, and turned not aside right nor left, so he always walketh forward in a straight line and was eventually never seen again. Now a priest, Hilkiah, read the book of the Lord unto Josiah. It sayeth servants shall have a rise, a five-day week, four weeks' holiday a year. 'Oh, my life,' moaned Josiah and he rent his clothes.

38. It was a beautiful day so the Lord sayeth to Josiah, 'Thou shall be gathered into thy grave in peace.'

'I'm not dead yet,' sayeth Josiah.

'Don't worry, you soon will be when you're buried. I don't wish thine eyes to see the evil I will do to this land.'

'Can't I stay and see it?' sayeth Josiah.

So the Lord sayeth, 'I'll put thy death on hold.' Then the Lord smote the land, he causeth the brothels to burn and the women scream to their clients, 'For God's sake, hurry up, we're on fire.'

39. At this time the king of Babylon was Nebuchadnezzar, and the Lord sent against him bands of Chaldees, bands of Syrians and bands from Ammon; they were never successful and never got in the charts.

40. Finally, Josiah died, he was cremated and they threw his ashes in his bank manager's face.

41. Jehoiachin came to the throne; he was very short and had to stand on a chair to reach puberty. He had Hodges' disease and Hodges had his. He started to do evil, he putteth Araldite on door knobs and on toilet seats. The Lord was wrath. He maketh Nebuchadnezzar attack Jehoiachin and plunder the city taking the fish knives, and take king Jehoiachin as hostage and waiter.

THEN THERE WAS THE TIME OF DAVID, the Lord God spoke to him from an apple strudel; He sayeth, 'Build me a temple.' So David built it, he gave gold for all things gold, and silver for all things silver, gold candlesticks, silver candlesticks, gold for the table of shewbread, gold for the fleshhooks, all was gold, even the chariots of the cherubims. It was finished in the third month and king David declared bankrupt and the Lord blessed David and his overdraft. Then David gave the Lord a burnt offering, a thousand bullocks, a thousand rams, a thousand lambs, thus decimating all the flocks of Israel. David died at a great age, all that was left on his grave was the undertaker's bill. Now Solomon the Wise came to the throne, so he went to the temple to make a burnt offering to God, chicken and chips, because after his father David had finished, that's all that was left. A time came when king Solomon passed all the other kings of the earth in riches and wisdom, so he fainted. He goeth into the temple to thank the Lord, he mounted steps six cubits high and he knelt down, he raised his arms to heaven and went arse over tip, backwards.

2. When the Israelites received planning permission

the builders laid the foundation of the temple. The builders were very good at laying, they'd laid half the girls in the district. Now the priests blew their trumpets, clashed their cymbals and beat their drums, and from everywhere came cries of 'Noisy buggers'. And ancient men seeing the new temple wept with a loud voice, many shouted for joy, so that people could not discern the noise of the shouts of joy from noise of weeping; to solemnise the occasion it was called Noisy Buggers' day, and the Lord blessed it. Then the Lord was woe again. He sayeth, 'Woe to them that work evil in thy bed, at night and in the morning light they practise it, it is in the power of their right hand, if they go on doing it they will go blind. Thou shall sow, but shall not reap, thou shall tread the olives, but no oil will come, thou shall tread the grapes but no wine will come.'

'And if thou callest the fire brigade, verily they will not come. And, lo, there began a recession and it lasted and lasted and lasted and lasted.

He just wanted a decent book to read ...

Not too much to ask, is it? It was in 1935 when Allen Lane, Managing Director of Bodley Head Publishers, stood on a platform at Exeter railway station looking for something good to read on his journey back to London. His choice was limited to popular magazines and poor-quality paperbacks – the same choice faced every day by the vast majority of readers, few of whom could afford hardbacks. Lane's disappointment and subsequent anger at the range of books generally available led him to found a company – and change the world.

'We believed in the existence in this country of a vast reading public for intelligent books at a low price, and staked everything on it'
Sir Allen Lane, 1902–1970, founder of Penguin Books

The quality paperback had arrived – and not just in bookshops. Lane was adamant that his Penguins should appear in chain stores and tobacconists, and should cost no more than a packet of cigarettes.

Reading habits (and cigarette prices) have changed since 1935, but Penguin still believes in publishing the best books for everybody to enjoy. We still believe that good design costs no more than bad design, and we still believe that quality books published passionately and responsibly make the world a better place.

So wherever you see the little bird – whether it's on a piece of prize-winning literary fiction or a celebrity autobiography, political tour de force or historical masterpiece, a serial-killer thriller, reference book, world classic or a piece of pure escapism – you can bet that it represents the very best that the genre has to offer.

Whatever you like to read – trust Penguin.